日英対訳

恋と人生に前向きになる英語100

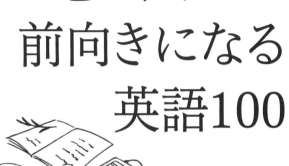

100 Keys of Love

Vicki Bennett = 著

かとゆみ = 訳

IBCパブリッシング

装　　幀＝高橋玲奈

編集協力＝iTEP Japan

本書の英語テキストは、弊社から刊行されたラダーシリーズ『100 Keys of Love』と共通です。

ポジティブな英語を聞いて、ポジティブな自分になる

英語とポジティブ思考を同時に手に入れる、
ヴィッキーのセラピー・イングリッシュ

可能性に満ちた時代を生きる女性たち

　現代は女性にとってわくわくするような時代です。多くの機会に恵まれ、さまざまな知識や情報にも簡単にアクセスすることができます。かつてないほど、皆が女性の声に耳を傾けています。組織のリーダー、政府の高官として世界的に活躍する女性も多く、女性の取締役も増えています。学校、仕事、パートナー、子供を持つかどうか——現代の女性は、そのような人生における選択の多くを、自分でできる時代に生きています。

　歴史的に見て、このように多くの選択肢が女性自身にゆだねられた時代はありません。私たちは自分を表現し、自分が望んだ人生を作り上げることができるのです。自己実現と成功、その希望あふれる時代に私たちは生きているのです。しかし逆から見れば、誰に頼ることもできない時代に女性は投げ出されてしまったともいえるでしょう。本書の執筆にあたり、私はこのような今までにない女性の環境に焦点をあて、アドバイスをしています。

つきない恋の悩み、人生への悩み

　私は、コンサルタントという仕事柄、何百人もの女性の悩みを聞いてきました。はたから見て、成功していると思える人でも、恋愛でひどく

悩み、自分は幸福でないと感じている人はたくさんいます。逆に、それらの悩みを自分自身で上手に解決していける人もいます。

　礼儀正しい人、ユーモアがある人、不安定な人、情熱的な人、明るい人、やさしい人、怒りっぽい人、落ち込みがちの人、自信満々の人、シャイな人、幸福な人、悲しんでいる人、嫉妬深い人……そんなさまざまな側面を持つ女性たちですが、共通する性質が1つだけあります。それは、「好奇心」です。愛に、人生に、自分の可能性に、将来の選択に対する好奇心。それが女性の誰もが持っている性格ではないでしょうか。

　女性たちは皆、自分への好奇心にあふれています。だからこそ、皆が愛を探し、自分とは何かを探し続けています。本書の各章は、そのための道しるべとなっています。そして100のメッセージは、より豊かでポジティブな考え方ができるようにあなたを助けてくれるでしょう。この本で、自分とは何か、人生の中で自分が得たいものは何か、それ以外に何を見つけることができるのかを、探していただきたいと思います。

ヴィッキー・ベネット

本書の効果的な使い方

ポジティブな英語を何度も聞こう

　試験のため、資格のため、日常会話のため……今までそれぞれの目的から、多くの教材をリスニング、ヒアリングのテキストに使用されてきたことと思います。その多くが、ニュースや新聞といった報道、映画やドラマの一場面、小説などの物語、ネイティブ同士の会話などではなかったでしょうか？　そしてその英語は、あなたの心に響くものでしたか？

　日本語の本をとっても分かるように、本のメッセージが心に届かなければ、どのような文章も生きた言葉として自分に吸収されることはありません。朝読んだ新聞記事の文章をもう思い出せないように（ましてやもう一度読みたいとは思わないように）、私たちが思っている以上にヒアリングやリスニングにおける「メッセージ性」は重要です。メッセージが強く、自分に届くものであればあるほど、あなたの耳はその言葉をとらえることができるのです。そして、繰り返し聞こうという気持ちも起こってくるはずです。

　本書はオーストラリアで人気のコンサルタントであり、若い人たちのカウンセラーも務めるヴィッキー・ベネットが、日本の読者、とりわけ女性に向けて書き下ろしたものです。恋の悩みを中心として、困難の多い現代を、いかに自分らしく生きていくかが主題となっています。日本人の読者向けに、難しい単語を使っていないというのは、私たち学習者にとって大きな助けとなります。そして、彼女の本の人気の大きな理由として、文章によるセラピー効用があります。本書の英文は私たちの心を癒やし、勇気づけ、前に進ませる気づきに満ちています。

　英語の実力を上げるために英語を聞かねばならないとしたら、無味乾燥

な文章の羅列を頭に流し込むより、ポジティブで明日の元気にもとになる英語を自分にプレゼントしてはいかがでしょうか？　英語の実力とポジティブ思考を同時に手に入れること、それが本書の目標です。

何度も繰り返し聞き、メッセージに触れる

　この本は中学レベルの、やさしい英単語を使って執筆されています。初めからすべての文章を理解する必要はありません。何度か音声を聞いているうちに、メッセージは自然と理解されるようになるでしょう。またそれが英語であるからこそ、あなたの脳にとってもインパクトのあるメッセージとなるはずです。

　英語はポジティブな言語です。そして英語で書かれた本書のポジティブなメッセージは、あなたの心にしみ込み、あなたを元気にし、気持ちを前向きにしてくれるはずです。

学習方法

　皆さんのレベルや目的によって、本書の使い方はさまざまです。もちろん下記の方法を組み合わせることも可能です。ぜひご自身の好きな方法を見つけ、本書をご活用ください。

【方法1】

(まず本文を読む)　⇒　(音声を繰り返し聞く)

【方法2】

(まず音声を聞く)　⇒　(本文の内容が聞き取れているか 訳を見て確認する)　⇒　(もう一度 音声を聞く)

【方法3】

(繰り返し音声を聞く)　⇒　(意味がわかってきたところで本を開く)

【方法4】

音声を聞きながら本文を見る
（訳で内容を確認する） ➡ 音声を繰り返し聞く

【方法5】

音声を繰り返し聞き、音に慣れる ➡ 本文を見ながら音声の後ろについて
読む（シャドーイング）

音声について

　本書の録音は、Vanessa Anthony さんによるものです。彼女の声はとてもやさしく、心に響く特別なもの。柔らかい声で、聞く人の心を癒やしてくれます。

- ●アメリカ英語（女性ナレーター）
- ●全収録時間　　約1時間56分
- ●スピード　　　ナチュラル・イングリッシュより少し遅め
- ●収録内容　　　本文の英語テキスト

無料音声一括ダウンロード

　本書の朗読音声（MP3形式）を下記URLとQRコードから無料でPCなどに一括ダウンロードすることができます。

https://www.ibcpub.co.jp/audio_dl/0686/

※ダウンロードしたファイルはZIP形式で圧縮されていますので、
　解凍ソフトが必要です。
※PCや端末、ソフトウェアの操作・再生方法については、編集部ではお答えできません。製造元にお問い合わせいただくか、インターネットで検索するなどして解決してください。

本書の構成

本文について

　この本で、ぜひたくさんのポジティブな単語や表現に接してください。そして自分の中に、ポジティブな英語表現のストックを増やしておきましょう。

サマリーについて

　日本語で書かれたサマリーは、聞く前、もしくは聞きながら目を通しておくと、リスニングの手助けとなるでしょう。また、まずリスニングをしてから、文章の主題を理解できていたかを確認するツールとしてもお使いいただけます。

日本語訳について

　自然な日本語で書かれています。本文の内容が聞き取れているか確認し、英文の理解を深め、さらにリスニング力をアップさせるために活用してください。

語句解説について

　難しいと思われる単語や表現を本文理解の助けとなるように示しています。学習本のように「look forward to -ing 〜を楽しみに待つ」といった表記の仕方ではなく、「look forward to being in love 恋愛に期待する」というように、直接本文の翻訳にあたる解説を入れています。

スマホからページごとの
MP3音声を聞くことが
できます。

本文

日本人読者向けのやさしい英語
で文章が書かれています。
読み上げは、ナチュラル・イン
グリッシュよりほんの少し遅い
スピードです。

サマリー

本文の内容を短い日本語でま
とめています。英文を聞き取
る際のガイドになります。

---

1 Allow For Love

It is natural to **look forward to being in love** and to being loved.
But if you **expect love too much**, if you hope too hard, you may
change how you act day-to-day. If you do not act in your natural
way, you may make it harder for love to come to you. You may
send the wrong signs to men about who you are that make it
harder for them to like you.

Even though you might not realize it, everyone shows little signs
to the other person about how they feel and what they think. Do
not hope too much for friendship or **romance**, be yourself and
allow love to find you.

Keep the goal of a romance in your mind but do not spend a lot
of time thinking about it or changing your natural way of acting.
Keep the door open for romance, but do not look at every man
you meet and ask yourself if he is **Mr. Right**.

Let friendship and romance happen naturally.

look forward to being in love 恋愛に期待する   expect love too much 恋愛
に期待しすぎる   romance ロマンス   allow love to find you 愛にあなたを見つ
けさせる   Mr. Right 理想の人

～ 24 ～

---

1. 恋に備える

恋をしたいと思うのは当然です。
ただ、期待をしすぎてはいけません。
あなたに必要なことは、
いつでも恋ができるよう準備をしておくこと、
そして自分らしくあることです。

【日本語訳】
　恋をしたい、愛されたい、と思うのは当然のことです。でも、
恋に期待しすぎたり強く望みすぎたりすると、日々のふるまい
が変わってしまうことも。自分らしくふるまえないことで、恋
を遠ざけてしまうこともあります。あなた自身について間違っ
たサインを男性に送ってしまい、好かれにくくなるからです。
　自分では気づいてなくても、誰もが自分の気持ちや考えにつ
いて相手に小さなサインを送っています。友情やロマンスを求
めすぎず、自分らしくふるまい、恋のほうからあなたを見つけ
てくれるのを待ちましょう。
　理想のロマンスを思い描くのは良いけれど、そのことばかり
考えたり、自分らしいふるまいを変えたりはしないこと。ロマ
ンスを受け入れる準備は万全に。でも、男性を見るたびに彼が
運命の人かどうかなんて考えてはいけません。
　友情とロマンスが自然に芽生えるのを待ちましょう。

～ 25 ～

語句解説

難しいと思われる単語や表現に
対して、本文の理解につながる
意味や訳を入れています。

日本語訳

日本語訳を確認することで、
英文の理解を深め、リスニン
グ力をさらにアップさせま
しょう。

SECTION 1
FINDING LOVE
恋を見つける

SECTION 2
FALLING IN LOVE
恋に落ちる

SECTION 3
WHEN LOVE IS NEW
始まったばかり

SECTION 4
KEEPING THE FLAME OF LOVE ALIVE AND HEALTHY
愛の炎を絶やさず健全に保つ

SECTION 5
THROUGHOUT IT ALL
どんなときでも

SECTION 6
WHEN LOVE IS OVER
愛が終わったら

SECTION 7
LOVING YOURSELF
自分を好きになる

恋と人生に
前向きになる英語100

100 Keys of Love

SECTION

1

FINDING LOVE

恋を見つける

'Take spring when it comes and rejoice.
Take happiness when it comes and rejoice.
Take love when it comes and rejoice.'
Carl Ewald

「春が訪れ心踊るとき、春を楽しみなさい。
幸せが訪れ心踊るとき、幸せを楽しみなさい。
恋が訪れ心踊るとき、恋を楽しみなさい」

カール・エヴァルト

1 *Allow For Love*

It is natural to **look forward to being in love** and to being loved. But if you **expect love too much**, if you hope too hard, you may change how you act day-to-day. If you do not act in your natural way, you may make it harder for love to come to you. You may send the wrong signs to men about who you are that make it harder for them to like you.

Even though you might not realize it, everyone shows little signs to the other person about how they feel and what they think. Do not hope too much for friendship or **romance**, be yourself and **allow love to find you**.

Keep the goal of a romance in your mind but do not spend a lot of time thinking about it or changing your natural way of acting. Keep the door open for romance, but do not look at every man you meet and ask yourself if he is **Mr. Right**.

Let friendship and romance happen naturally.

look forward to being in love 恋愛に期待する　　expect love too much 恋愛に期待しすぎる　　romance ロマンス　　allow love to find you 愛にあなたを見つけさせる　　Mr. Right 理想の人

1. 恋に備える

恋をしたいと思うのは当然です。
ただ、期待をしすぎてはいけません。
あなたに必要なことは、
いつでも恋ができるよう準備をしておくこと、
そして自分らしくあることです。

【日本語訳】
　恋をしたい、愛されたい、と思うのは当然のことです。でも、恋に期待しすぎたり強く望みすぎたりすると、日々のふるまいが変わってしまうことも。自分らしくふるまえないことで、恋を遠ざけてしまうこともあります。あなた自身について間違ったサインを男性に送ってしまい、好かれにくくなるからです。

　自分では気づいてなくても、誰もが自分の気持ちや考えについて相手に小さなサインを送っています。友情やロマンスを求めすぎず、自分らしくふるまい、恋のほうからあなたを見つけてくれるのを待ちましょう。

　理想のロマンスを思い描くのは良いけれど、そのことばかり考えたり、自分らしいふるまいを変えたりはしないこと。ロマンスを受け入れる準備は万全に。でも、男性を見るたびに彼が運命の人かどうかなんて考えてはいけません。

　友情とロマンスが自然に芽生えるのを待ちましょう。

2 *Falling In Love*

Falling in love is a very special feeling; it is exciting, **pleasing**, and perhaps very new to you. Sometimes it also **makes you worry about the future**. It asks for new trust and **new sharing** and it makes you think about your sense of control over your life. Suddenly **your life seems to be rushing off** in new ways without you having control over it.

There is something special about the romance that comes with falling in love, with the opening of your heart to another person. Your dreams will change and your thoughts will also change; you will dream about what may happen with your new love and with the person you are falling in love with, and your thoughts will turn so often to that person. What is he doing right now? What is he thinking?

What you do each day will also change. You will plan with this new person to meet for coffee or to sit in the park. You will want to think ahead and make special plans, or to find a special moment such as buying a card to say how much you love that person.

Enjoy these **emotions** and thoughts; it is a very special time in your life. Let your whole being enjoy the beauty of falling in love.

---

pleasing 楽しい   makes you worry about the future 将来の不安を感じる
new sharing ゼロから分かち合う   your life seems to be rushing off 人生が急
展開する   emotions 感情

2. 恋に落ちる

恋をすることで、あなたの毎日が、将来の夢が、
変化していくかもしれません。
恋をするというのは特別なことです。
まずはその感情を思い切り楽しみましょう。

【日本語訳】

　恋に落ちるのはとても特別な感情です。ワクワクして楽しく、あなたにとって全く初めての感情かもしれません。将来の不安を感じることもあるでしょう。ゼロから信頼関係を築き、ゼロから分かち合うことが求められ、どのように人生の舵を切れば良いか考えさせられるでしょう。突然、人生が新たな方向へ急展開し、コントロールが効かなくなるからです。

　恋をして相手に心を開くことから始まるロマンスには、何か特別なものがあります。将来の夢が変わり、考え方も変わるでしょう。新しい恋のゆくえや、恋に落ちた相手との未来を夢見て、その人のことを四六時中考えるようになります。彼は今何をしているんだろう？　何を考えているんだろう、と。

　あなたの日々の行動も変化します。新しい彼とのカフェや公園デートの予定を立てたり、特別なデートプランを考えたり、彼に気持ちを伝えるためにメッセージカードを買う、といった特別な瞬間もあるでしょう。

　こうした感情や思考を楽しみましょう。それはあなたの人生において、とても特別な時間です。恋をする素晴らしさを全身で味わいましょう。

3 *Perfect Love?*

Love is a very special feeling. Much is talked about romance as being perfect, but having that special feeling all the time is not possible. Someone else cannot make you feel special all of the time and you can't make someone else happy all of the time.

Women will be disappointed if they **search for the 'perfect' love,** where everything is great and the other person is thinking and **caring about** you all the time. It's easy to **lose your sense of reality** and come to hope too much for this kind of love, as your heart will be excited and your hopes will be high.

If you can have good feelings about yourself when you are falling in love, if you can care about and love yourself, if you can accept that love isn't perfect all the time, then you will allow love to happen in a more natural and caring way.

---

women will be disappointed 女性は失望させられる   search for the 'perfect' love 「完璧な」恋愛を求める   (is) caring about 大切にしている   lose your sense of reality 現実を見失う

3. 完璧な恋愛？

完璧な恋愛などありません。
そのことを受け入れたとき、
もっと自然なやさしい形で恋愛が始まるのです。

【日本語訳】
　恋愛はとても特別な感情です。完璧な恋愛について語られる
のをよく耳にしますが、最初の特別な感情をずっと持ち続ける
ことは不可能です。誰かがあなたを常に特別な気持ちにさせる
ことはできないし、あなたが誰かを常に幸せにすることもでき
ません。
　何もかもが素晴らしく、相手があなたのことを常に想って大
切にしてくれる「完璧な」恋愛を求めてしまうと、女性は失望
させられるでしょう。恋をすると現実を見失い、完璧な恋愛に
期待しがちです。恋をすると胸が高鳴り、期待が高まるからです。
　恋をしている自分に良い感情を抱き、自分を大切にして自分
を愛し、常に完璧な恋愛などないということを受け入れたとき、
もっと自然なやさしい形で恋愛が始まるのです。

4 *What Men Want*

It is impossible to understand what goes on in someone else's mind. Women often try to guess what men want, without asking them.

Never try to guess what a man might want in a relationship. If you are in a relationship or starting a relationship, ask him. Ask gently, let him know that you care about him and wish to care for his needs.

Many men are not very confident about relationships and do not have a clear idea about what they want. Most men will welcome being asked and will **welcome the opportunity to talk** about their needs. Such discussion may also start him talking about your needs in a relationship.

There is no one answer to the question about what men want. Many things are written and said about what men want, especially in popular magazines and on TV. Most of these things are wrong. Every man is different and every man's needs are different.

Try not to listen to talk about what men want from other people or from TV or magazines. If you need to know what your man wants, ask him.

---

many men are not very confident about relationships 多くの男性は恋愛にあまり自信がない   welcome the opportunity to talk 話す機会を喜ぶ

4. 男性が望むこと

彼が望んでいることを知りたいなら、
想像するのではなく、質問することです。

【日本語訳】

　他人の頭の中を理解することは不可能です。女性は男性が求めていることを、本人に聞かずに推測しようとしがち。

　男性が2人の関係に求めていることは何かを、推測しようとするのはやめましょう。交際中や交際を始めたばかりの場合は、彼に直接聞きましょう。やさしく聞いて、あなたが彼の気持ちを気にかけていて、彼が何を求めているかを知りたいと思っていることを伝えましょう。

　多くの男性は恋愛にあまり自信がなく、自分が何を求めているかよく分かっていません。ほとんどの男性は聞かれることを歓迎し、自分が求めていることについて話す機会を喜んで受け入れます。このような話し合いは、あなたが恋愛に求めることについて彼の方から話を振ってくれるきっかけになるかもしれません。

　男性が望むことは何か、という問いに対する答えは1つではありません。人気雑誌やテレビでは男性の欲求についてさまざまなことが語られていますが、ほとんどが間違っています。男性はみな違うし、求めるものも人それぞれです。

　男性が求めているものについて語る、他人やテレビ、雑誌に耳を傾けるのはやめましょう。彼が何を求めているか知りたいなら、彼に尋ねましょう。

5 *What Women Want*

What other women want should **not matter to you**. You are not the same as other women, you are you. The question is 'What is it you want?' and being able to **express** this is much more important.

What you are told about other women and their wants is probably not what you feel your needs are. It is **far too easy** to **allow your thinking to be changed** from what you really want to what others tell you that you should want. Often people copy their thoughts or hopes from people on TV, the Internet or magazines, and those hopes or thoughts are not really their own.

Think about what you want for yourself. **What will suit you**; make you happy or pleased with your life? What are your plans, your hopes; what is your picture of the future? Keep your own thoughts close to you and talk with your friends or your partner about your dreams and hopes, not the ideas that come from other people and magazines.

Are you clear about what you want? Take some time to think about this very important question. You may find that your thoughts about what you want will change over time; these thoughts will change and grow as time passes. Be prepared for such change. The important thing is to remember your own hopes and dreams, not those of someone else.

---

not matter to you あなたにとってはどうでもいい　express 表現する　far too easy あまりにも簡単に　allow your thinking to be changed 思考が塗り替えられる　what will suit you 何があなたに合っているのか

5. 女性が望むこと

あなたの欲しいものは、
他の人とは違うはずです。

【日本語訳】

　他の女性が求めているものはあなたにとってはどうでもいいはずです。あなたは他の女性と同じではなく、あなたはあなただからです。問題は「あなたが何を求めているか」であり、それを表現することのほうがずっと大切です。

　他の女性たちについてあなたが見聞きすることや、彼女たちが求めているものは、おそらくあなたが求めているものとは違うと感じるでしょう。それなのに、思考はあまりにも簡単に塗り替えられ、あなたが本当に求めているものが、あなたが求めていると他人が思うものに変わってしまうのです。自分の本当の望みや考えではないにもかかわらず、テレビやインターネット、雑誌で見る人たちの真似をしてしまう人がいかに多いことか。

　あなた自身が求めているものは何かを考えましょう。何があなたに合っているのか。あなたの人生に幸福や喜びをもたらすものは何か。あなたの計画や希望は？　あなたが思い描く未来とは？　あなた自身の考えをしっかりと持って、友人や彼と夢や希望について話し合いましょう。他人や雑誌から得たアイデアではなく。

　あなたは自分が何を望んでいるか分かっていますか？　この大切な問いについて、じっくりと考えてみましょう。すると、あなたの考えは時間とともに変化するということに気がつくでしょう。時間の経過とともに考えも変化し成長するものなのです。こうした変化に備えておきましょう。大切なのは、他人の希望や夢ではなく、自分自身の希望や夢を覚えておくことなのです。

6 *Keep In Touch With What's Real*

At times in your life you can easily believe things that are not real or true for you. Other people's ideas will **influence you**. Ideas can come into your mind that seem to be OK at the time but later you might ask yourself, 'Why did I think like that?'

This happens often in life. It is easy for this to happen. But you can find ways to keep joined with what's real and true for you.

One way is to stop every now and again and ask yourself some simple questions. 'Am I clear about what I am thinking? Are there any little things that worry me at the moment? Are any of my family and friends asking me questions that **upset me**?'

Another way is to ask your partner, a friend or someone in your family to sit with you and talk about your life. Ask someone you can trust. From time to time, talk with them about whether your life is meeting your hopes and vision. Talk about whether you are happy or not.

Encourage honesty within yourself. Work out your own way to keep in touch with what's real in your life.

---

keep in touch with ～に目を向ける   influence you あなたに影響を与える
upset me 私を動揺させる   Encourage honesty within yourself. 自分の心に正直になりましょう。

6. 現実的なことだけに目を向ける

**周りから影響を受けすぎてはいませんか。
何が大切なのか、じっくり考えましょう。**

【日本語訳】
　ときに人は、自分に当てはまらない非現実的なことでも簡単に信じてしまいます。他人のアイデアに影響されるのです。外から入ってきたアイデアは、そのときは良く思えても、あとになって「何であんなふうに考えたんだろう」と思うことになるでしょう。

　これはよくあることで、しかも簡単に起こります。そこで、自分に当てはまる現実的なことだけに目を向ける方法をご紹介しましょう。

　1つ目の方法は、ときどき、自分に簡単な質問をしてみることです。「自分が何を考えているか分かってる？　今、何か小さな心配事はある？　家族や友人の中に、私に嫌なことを聞いてくる人はいる？」など。

　もう1つの方法は、あなたの人生について彼や友人、家族の誰かとじっくり話し合うことです。あなたが信頼している人に頼みましょう。ときどき、彼らと一緒に、あなたが望み、思い描いたとおりの人生になっているかどうかを振り返ってみましょう。そして、あなたが幸せかどうかも。

　自分の心に正直に。自分に当てはまる現実的なことに目を向ける方法を見つけて実践しましょう。

7 *The Strength Of Being Alone*

Learn how to enjoy being in your own company. You can learn so much about yourself when you spend time alone, listening to your own thoughts. Get to know yourself as you would a close friend. Spend some time alone to get to know yourself better.

If you look for a relationship to fill an empty space within you it won't always make you happy. The person may not be who or what you think they are or you may not be who or what they really want.

If that space in you is filled with love for yourself then when you do find someone to love, the relationship can start from **strength and equality** rather than **needing and wanting** someone to make you happy. If you already like yourself, the other person liking or loving you is an added happy event.

Even if you are happy in a relationship, you may welcome having time alone from time to time.

---

strength and equality 強さと対等   needing and wanting 欲求や要望

7. ひとりでいる強さ

ひとりでいる時間はとても大切です。
自分と向き合い、
自分をもっと深く知るきっかけにもなります。

【日本語訳】
　　ひとりでいることを楽しむ方法を学びましょう。ひとりで過ごして心の声に耳を傾けると、自分をもっと深く知ることができます。親友のことを知るように、あなた自身を知りましょう。自分をもっと深く知るためにひとりで過ごす時間を作りましょう。

　　心の隙間を埋めるために恋人を探しても、幸せになれるとは限りません。相手はあなたが思っているような人ではないかもしれないし、あなたも相手が本当に求めている人ではないかもしれません。

　　心の隙間を自分自身への愛で埋めることができれば、愛する人に出逢ったとき、2人の関係は「自分を幸せにしてほしい」という欲求や要望ではなく、強さと対等な関係から始まるでしょう。あなたが自分を好きでいれば、相手に好かれることや愛されることは、ちょっとした嬉しい出来事でしかないのです。

　　幸せな恋愛をしている最中でも、たまにはひとりで過ごす時間を持つようにしましょう。

8 *Understand Yourself First*

Take time to understand yourself first. Most women don't think their own needs and feelings are important. It takes time and effort to **get to know yourself well**.

Think about what you want and how you feel. Take care that you do not let your thoughts and actions about another person pull you **ahead of getting to know yourself first**. The more you know and like yourself, the more chance the relationship has of success.

Your partner will want to get to know who you are, so it is important to have taken the time to work that out and to be clear about who you are and what you want. When you share this with another person they will be meeting the real you, the true you.

---

get to know yourself well 自分自身をよく知る   ahead of getting to know
yourself first 自分自身を知るより先に

8. まず自分を理解する

多くの女性は
自分のことを後まわしにしてしまいます。
あなた自身が何を求め、何を思っているのか。
自分のことをもっと知りましょう。

【日本語訳】
　まずは自分を理解するための時間を取りましょう。ほとんどの女性が自分自身の望みや気持ちを軽視しています。自分自身をよく知るためには時間と労力が必要です。

　あなた自身が何を求め、どう思っているのか考えましょう。自分自身を知るより先に、他人のことを考え、他人のために行動しないように注意してください。自分自身をもっと知って好きになればなるほど、恋愛がうまくいく可能性が高まります。

　彼はあなたがどんな人かを知りたがるでしょう。ですから、自分自身を知る時間を取って、あなたがどんな人で何を求めているのかを、あなた自身が分かっていることが大切です。それを相手に伝えることで、相手は本当のあなたに出会うことができるのです。

9 *Free Will*

Free will is your ability to make a decision by yourself for yourself. When you use free will you choose to do something, or not do something, because of your own thoughts and experiences.

The difference between animals and humans is a human's ability to make decisions and use their free will to choose the best thing to do at any moment.

Do you use your own free will in your relationships? Do you listen to your experience, your wisdom, your understanding of things and trust yourself to make the right decisions for your life? When you listen, **your own inner thoughts and feelings** guide you to know the very best thing for you to do.

Using free will is like exercising your body. If you don't exercise your body you will lose some of your strength and it may not work as well as it could. Free will needs to be used every day for it to be a strength in your life. Use it every day.

free will is your ability 自由意思はあなたの能力である　your own inner thoughts and feelings あなたの考えや気持ちを表す内なる声

9. 自由意思

**強く生きるためには、あなたの意思が大切です。
人生において、何をして、何をしないかは、
あなた自身の決断で選び取るものだからです。**

【日本語訳】
　自由意思とは、自分自身のために自分で意思決定をする能力です。自由意思を使うとき、人は自分の考えと経験に基づいて何かをする、もしくはしないことを選択します。
　動物と人との違いは、自由意思を使う能力にあります。人はどんな瞬間もベストな選択をするために意思決定をします。
　あなたは恋愛に自由意思を使っていますか？　自分の経験や知恵に耳を傾け、自分の理解力や判断力を信じて、あなたの人生にとって正しい決断をしていますか？　あなたの考えや気持ちを表す内なる声に耳を傾けると、その声はあなたにとってベストな選択ができるよう導いてくれます。
　自由意思を使うことは運動に似ています。身体を動かさなければ、一部の力が失われ、本来の機能を果たさなくなることがあります。自由意思も同じで、あなたの人生にとっての力となるには毎日使う必要があるのです。ですから、自由意思を毎日使いましょう。

10 *Fate*

Fate is often a word used to explain something that has happened that seems to be out of your control. Fate is the idea of something happening that is bigger or better than your own free will.

Some people **leave their whole lives up to fate** and some leave their love lives up to fate... Others believe they control their lives through free will. Get to know which of these two you use and trust.

Tuck, a young woman in her 20's, talked about fate and her boyfriend. 'When I met him, I knew it was fate. I wasn't meant to be at the bus stop. It wasn't a bus stop I had ever been to before. I was there because I was late and a friend dropped me there to catch my bus and I started talking to this man because he was waiting for a bus there also. So I met my boyfriend because of fate, so the relationship must have been meant to happen.'

Fate can be things happening that are **out of the ordinary** or happy accidents or something that seems really unusual. These things that are called fate can lead to happy relationships sometimes, sometimes not.

Fate may draw you together in the first place, but your free will to act and react **in certain ways** will be what keeps you together.

---

leave their whole lives up to fate 人生のすべてを運命に任せる　out of the
ordinary 日常からかけ離れた　in certain ways 何らかの形で

10. 運命

運命を生かせるかどうかは、あなた次第です。

【日本語訳】

運命とは、自分でコントロールできないと思われる出来事を説明するのによく使われる言葉です。運命とは、あなた自身の自由意思よりも強力で優位なものだと考えられています。

人生のすべてを運命に任せる人もいれば、恋愛を運命に任せる人もいます。一方で、自分の人生を自由意思によってコントロールしていると信じている人もいます。あなた自身が、運命と自由意思のどちらを信じ、どちらに人生を委ねるかを知りましょう。

タック(20代・女性)は、運命と恋人についてこう語っています。「彼に出会ったとき、私は運命を確信しました。もともと行く予定ではなかったバス停でしたし、それまで行ったこともありませんでしたから。私はたまたま予定に遅れていて、乗る予定だったバスに乗せるために友人がそのバス停まで送ってくれたんです。それで、私はそのバス停で同じくバスを待っていた彼と話し始めたんです。ですから、私が彼に出会ったのは運命なんです。2人はこうなる運命だったんです」

運命とは、日常からかけ離れた出来事や、嬉しい偶然、もしくはすごく珍しい出来事をいいます。運命と呼ばれるこれらの出来事は、幸せな関係につながることもあれば、そうでないこともあります。

最初に2人を引き合わせるのは運命かもしれませんが、自分が取るべき行動や反応を決める自由意思こそが2人をつなぎとめるのです。

SECTION
2
FALLING IN LOVE
恋に落ちる

'We waste time looking for the perfect lover,
instead of creating the perfect love.'
Tom Robbins

「我々は完璧な恋愛を生み出す代わりに、
完璧な恋人を探すために時間を無駄にしている」

トム・ロビンズ

11 *Romantic Love*

The idea of romantic love is a strongly held belief in most women. Many women dream of a man coming into their life and falling in love with them and everything being OK forever.

The dream of falling deeply in love easily and **living happily ever after** is common among women. This is not how it happens most of the time. Love can be difficult and painful at times and it can be hard to go on loving someone. After a time the first stage of romance can leave the relationship and change into a different kind of love and you may miss that new falling-in-love feeling. Some people just keep changing partners because they only want to feel that first falling-in-love feeling.

Most people **in long-term relationships** still enjoy romantic feelings from time to time—unlike new love, where **the first falling-in-love feeling** seems to be there all the time.

Falling in love is just the first step in a relationship, not the whole of the relationship. If you have **the courage to accept** that love changes over time, and journey through the changes in that love, a deeper love and pleasure will come from the relationship.

---

living happily ever after　一生幸せに暮らす　　in long-term relationships　長く交際を続けている　　the first falling-in-love feeling　恋に落ちたときの最初の気持ち　the courage to accept　受け入れる勇気

11. ロマンチックな恋愛

恋に落ちたときだけが、
恋愛のすべてではありません。
出会った頃のときめきはなくても、
その後には形を変えた大きな愛や喜びが
あなたを待っているのです。

【日本語訳】
　　多くの女性がロマンチックな恋愛を強く信じています。自分の人生に突然、素敵な人が現れて恋に落ち、一生幸せになれると夢見ている女性が少なくありません。

　　たやすく深い恋に落ちて一生幸せに暮らすという夢は、女性が共通して抱く夢です。でも、たいていの場合、こうはいきません。恋愛は難しく、ときに痛みを伴うもの。誰かを愛し続けることも容易ではありません。時が経てば、ロマンスの最初のステージは終わり、異なるかたちの愛に変わります。そして、恋に落ちたときの最初の気持ちを再び味わいたいと思うものです。恋に落ちたときの気持ちを味わいたいがためだけに、パートナーをコロコロ変える人もいます。

　　長く交際を続けているカップルでもときどき、ロマンチックな感情を抱くことはありますが、これは恋に落ちたときの最初の気持ちがずっと続くように思える交際初期とは異なる感情です。

　　恋に落ちることは男女の交際における最初のステップにすぎません。恋愛は時とともに変化するものだということを受け入れる勇気を持ち、その変化を経験すれば、2人の関係からより深い愛と喜びが生まれるでしょう。

12 *Enjoy Your New Love*

There is no special way to love someone, but some people find it difficult to **open their hearts to love**.

'I was always fearful of opening myself up to love. I had seen my mother get hurt over and over again as I was growing up and I didn't have much trust in relationships. So when I met someone I liked I would not open my heart and they would see this as me not being interested in them and walk away from me and any kind of relationship with me. It was hard for me just to be open and take a chance.'

Ono

Being in the moment with that special person, smiling and being present for them is a great start. Opening your heart to the other person is **a positive way to find the love** in your heart.

---

open their hearts to love 恋愛に心を開く　　a positive way to find the love 愛を見つけるポジティブな方法

12. 新しい恋を楽しむ

心を開くことが難しいこともあります。
でもそうすることで、
新しい恋はスタートするのです。

【日本語訳】

　人を愛するのに特別な方法などありませんが、恋愛に心を開くのが難しいと感じる人もいます。

「私は怖がってずっと恋愛に心を開けずにいました。母が何度も何度も傷ついているのを子供の頃から見ていたので、恋愛を信じることができなかったのです。だから、好きな人ができても心を開かず、相手は私が彼に興味がないと思って、私と距離を置いて関係を一切断ってしまうことがよくありました。心を開いてチャンスに賭けてみることが私には難しかったのです」

オノ

　まずは手始めに、特別な人と一緒に過ごし、笑顔でそばにいることから始めましょう。相手に心を開くことは、心の中に芽生えた愛を見つけるポジティブな方法です。

13 *Open Your Heart*

Many women are afraid to open their heart and trust another person **just in case they are hurt**. The risk may seem to be high; if you love someone, you **take the risk of being hurt or rejected**.

Some people ask us what it is like to really open your heart to someone. Adrienne told us this story. 'To open my heart for me is like when my four-year-old niece comes running up the stairs to say, "Hi." I see her and my heart is full of love and happiness. That to me is opening my heart. To just feel open and loving and **not expect anything in return**.'

Opening your heart to love and another person **takes courage**. There is always a risk that love will not succeed and you will be hurt, but falling in love without opening your heart is like having sushi without wasabi. One doesn't really work without the other.

just in case they are hurt 傷つくのを恐れて　　take the risk of being hurt or rejected 傷ついたり拒まれたりするリスクを負う　　not expect anything in return 何も見返りを求めない　　takes courage 勇気がいる

13. 心を開く

**人を愛すれば、傷つくこともあります。
これ以上傷つかないために、
心を閉ざしてはいませんか。**

【日本語訳】
　多くの女性が傷つくのを恐れて、心を開いて人を信じることを怖がっています。リスクは高く感じるかもしれませんが、誰かを愛するには、傷ついたり拒まれたりするリスクを負うものです。

　本当の意味で人に心を開くとはどういう感じなのかと私たちに尋ねる人もいます。エイドリアンがこんな話をしてくれました。「私にとって心を開く瞬間とは、4歳の姪っ子が私に挨拶するために階段を駆け上がって来たときです。『ハーイ！』と言う彼女を見て、私の心は愛と幸せでいっぱいになります。これが私にとって心を開くということです。ただ心を開いて愛情を感じ、何も見返りを求めないことです」

　好きな人や他人に心を開くのは勇気がいることです。恋愛がうまくいかず、傷つくリスクがつきまとうからです。でも、心を開かずに恋をすることは、ワサビのない寿司のようなもの。どちらが欠けてもうまくいかないのです。

14 *Listen To Yourself*

It can be difficult when you are falling in love to keep your mind clear and open to hear **your own inner wisdom**.

Love can make it difficult to make up your mind about what to do and what not to do. Sometimes you will want to ask someone else about what you should do. If you do this, remember that mostly they will tell you what they would do in the same situation. Hardly ever does the other person think about what is really best for you.

Let's say you tell a friend that you want to live with your boyfriend and that you are leaving home to do this. For them, it may seem to be the worst choice in the world and very stressful and they will advise you not to do it. They will talk about their fears and their worries.

They might say, 'You are doing the wrong thing, moving in with him,' or plant **the seed of doubt** by asking, 'Are you sure you know what you're doing?' What they really mean to say is, 'The thought of doing that makes me feel uneasy because I couldn't do it, so don't talk with me about doing it.' They mostly give their view.

Trust and listen to the advice from others, but always make your own decisions, following your own inner wisdom. If you listen to your feelings, your inner wisdom will guide you to solve your own issues and problems.

---

your own inner wisdom あなた自身の内なる声　　**the seed of doubt** 疑問の種

14. 心の声を聞く

**人のアドバイスに惑わされず、
自分自身で決めることが大切です。**

【日本語訳】
　恋に落ちると、頭の中を整理してあなた自身の内なる声に耳を傾けることが難しくなることがあります。

　恋愛中は、するべきこととしてはいけないことの判断がつきづらくなるのです。どうすればいいのか人に聞きたくなることもあるでしょう。でも、これをすると、たいてい人は自分がその状況に立ったときにどうするかを答えます。あなたにとって何が本当にベストかを考えてくれることはほとんどありません。

　家を出て彼と同棲したいと友人に話したとしましょう。友人にとってそれがとてもストレスの溜まる最悪の選択だとしたら、同棲をやめるようあなたにアドバイスをするでしょう。そして、自分の不安や心配事をあなたに話すでしょう。

　「彼と同棲するなんて、あなたは間違ったことをしようとしている」と言うかもしれないし、「自分が何をしようとしているか分かっているの？」と疑問をぶつけてくるかもしれません。でも友人が本当に言いたいのは、「同棲なんて考えただけで不安だわ。そんなこと私にはできないもの。だから私に同棲の話なんかしないで」ということなのです。

　他人のアドバイスを信じて耳を傾けることは大切ですが、常にあなたの心の声に従って、自分自身で決めるようにしましょう。自分の気持ちに耳を傾ければ、問題を解決できるよう心の声が導いてくれます。

15 *Commit With Passion*

Passion can easily be lost when you get used to each other in a relationship. Talking, listening and spending time together are all ways to **reconnect with the passion** you felt at the start of a relationship.

Connect with your passion by having more fun, being warm and close, sharing your thoughts of love, thinking kindly and being caring for your partner. Plan things to create this passion: plan surprises, special dates or **outings together**, touch more, laugh more, and do things for the other person that they are not expecting. This is how you create more passion in your life.

---

commit with passion 情熱を維持する   reconnect with the passion 情熱を取り戻す   outings together 一緒に出かける

15. 情熱を維持する努力

情熱を維持するには、努力が必要です。
サプライズや特別なデートの
プランを立てましょう。
彼が予想もしなかったことを計画してみましょう。

【日本語訳】
　交際する中でお互いに慣れてくると、情熱は簡単に失われて
しまいます。話したり、相手の話を聞いたり、一緒に過ごした
りすることは、つき合い始めた頃の情熱を取り戻す良い方法で
す。
　彼ともっと一緒に楽しいことをしたり、そばで温まったり、
恋愛に対する考えを話し合ったり、相手を思いやってやさしく
したりすることで、情熱を維持しましょう。情熱を生み出すた
めに、サプライズや特別なデート、お出かけの計画を立てたり、
もっと触れ合い、もっと笑い、相手が予想もしなかったことを
してみましょう。そうすれば、人生にもっと情熱が生まれるで
しょう。

16 *Take Your Time*

It takes time to get to know another person well; possibly a whole lifetime. Make the time to get to know someone well first before you make the choice to be with them forever. Don't **rush into a serious relationship** too fast. Sometimes the person you fall in love with may not be the type you would have expected to love. It can be very surprising who you fall in love with.

When you are first in love it is very easy not to notice things about the other person that you may not like. Love has a way of making you **blind to the other person's faults**.

The other person may be getting used to his own feelings; his feelings may be new to him also. He may need to match these feeling with yours and need time to do this. When you take your time to get to know someone well it helps friendship to grow between you and gives your relationship a good chance to be a success.

---

rush into a serious relationship　焦って深い関係になる　　blind to the other person's faults　相手の欠点が全く見えない

16. 時間をかける

相手を知るには、時間がかかります。
焦って先に進もうとしないことです。

【日本語訳】

　相手をよく知るには時間がかかります。一生かかることも。
生涯を共にすることを決める前に、時間をかけてまずは相手を
よく知りましょう。焦って深い関係になることは禁物です。あ
なたが恋に落ちる相手は、あなたにとって意外なタイプの人か
もしれません。驚くような相手に恋をすることもあります。

　恋に落ちたときは相手の嫌なところに気づかないものです。
恋をすると相手の欠点が全く見えなくなります。

　相手は自分自身の気持ちに慣れ始めたところかもしれないし、
彼にとっても初めての気持ちかもしれません。自分の気持ちと
あなたの気持ちのつり合いを取りたいと思っていて、そのため
に時間が必要な場合もあります。時間をかけて相手をよく知る
と、2人の間に友情が生まれ、関係がうまくいく可能性が高ま
ります。

17 Check Reality

How do you check that your relationship is what you think it is? When love is new and strong and passionate it is hard to stop and check your feelings deeply. If your thoughts become unclear and you don't know if your relationship is right for you, this is the time to give yourself a reality check.

'I was so in love I just went along with everything my boyfriend wanted. I had a small feeling that something wasn't right in our relationship, but I just didn't want to look too closely at it for fear it may **unravel the whole of the relationship**. It turned out he had a wife and child in another town and I was **just a bit of fun to him**.'

Tay

Take the time to talk and listen. Ask the hard questions to really get to know the other person.

unravel the whole of the relationship　関係が完全にだめになる　　just a bit of
fun to him　彼にとってただの遊びである

17. 現実を見つめる

少しでも疑問を感じたら、
現実を見つめる努力をしましょう。

【日本語訳】
　彼との関係が、あなたが思っているとおりかどうかを確認する方法は？　つき合い始めたばかりで、恋心と情熱が強いときには、立ち止まって自分の気持ちをじっくりと確認することは難しいもの。考えがまとまらなくなって、今の関係があなたにとって正しいかどうか分からなくなったら、現実を見つめるときです。

　「私は恋に夢中で、彼が求めるものすべてに同意していました。交際中、ちょっと変だなと感じたことはあったのですが、深追いしたくはありませんでした。2人の関係が完全にだめになってしまうのではと恐れたからです。あとで分かったことですが、彼には他の街に妻子がいて、彼にとって私はただの遊びだったのです」
                                                                    テイ

　時間を取って相手と話し合いましょう。あえて聞きづらい質問をして相手を知りましょう。

18 Don't Rush Love

When you rush into a relationship it can blind you to the other person as they really are and you may lose contact with your own feelings and values. Everyone needs time to think about their own needs and about what the other person is really like and to get to know them.

Find out about the other person—the things they think are important to them, the things they love and hate, like and dislike. **Put your feelings on hold** until you have worked out more about them.

It can be hard to do this because passion and love can be very strong and you may not want to go slowly. You may not see everything there is about the other person. It is very important to balance passion with getting to know the other person.

put your feelings on hold　気持ちを抑える

18. 恋は焦らず

焦らずに。
情熱に振り回されてはいけません。

【日本語訳】
　　焦って恋愛関係に走ると、相手が本当はどんな人かが見えなくなり、自分自身の気持ちや価値観を見失いがちです。自分自身が何を求めているのか、相手が本当はどんな人なのかを考え、相手のことを知るには時間が必要です。
　　相手のことを知りましょう。彼が大切だと考えていること（もの）、好きなこと（もの）と嫌いなこと（もの）など。彼のことをもっと深く知るまで、自分の気持ちを抑えましょう。
　　情熱や恋心はとても強く、ゆっくり前に進みたいとは思わないでしょうから、これは難しいことかもしれません。相手のあらゆる面を見ることができなくなるでしょう。情熱と相手を知ること、そのバランスがとても大切です。

SECTION

3

WHEN LOVE IS NEW
始まったばかり

'*We can only learn to love by loving.*'
Iris Murdoch

「愛することでしか愛は学べない」

アイリス・マードック

19 *Understand Each Other*

Everyone is different. There are no two people who have the same likes or the same dislikes. Each person has had their own life which is different from everyone else's. Your partner or boyfriend will probably have had a very different life than you. Sometimes that is just the thing that brings you together **in the first place**.

The only way you can learn to understand about another person is to ask them about themselves and to really listen to them when you tell you. **Try to picture what their life has been like** and understand where they have come from. When you listen to someone **with all your attention** you will understand them better and they will respect you more. They in turn may listen to you more when you choose to speak.

---

in the first place そもそも　try to picture what their life has been like どんな人生を歩んできたのかを想像する　with all your attention 最大の注意を払って

19. 互いを理解する

ひとりとして同じ人はいません。
相手を知るためには、
質問し、話を聞くことです。

【日本語訳】
　ひとりとして同じ人はいません。好きなもの嫌いなものが全く同じ人も2人といません。誰もが他人とは異なる人生を歩んできています。あなたのパートナーや恋人も、おそらくあなたとは全然違う人生を歩んできているでしょう。そもそもそれが、2人を引き寄せた原因であることも。
　相手を理解する唯一の方法は、相手のことを本人に尋ね、話してくれたときには真剣に耳を傾けることです。どんな人生を歩んできたのかを想像し、どんな環境で育ってきたかを理解するよう努めましょう。相手の話に全力で耳を傾ければ、相手のことをもっとよく理解することができ、相手もあなたのことをもっと尊重してくれるでしょう。そして相手も、あなたが話そうと決めたときに、もっと耳を傾けてくれるかもしれません。

20 *Grow The Relationship*

When you are in love and love is new, there can be a feeling that life is moving quickly and everything is rushing forward. There can be much excitement in your heart and your mind, and this is great. But it is very easy to let **this excitement carry you along** without thinking about where the relationship is going and how it is to be carried forward.

When this happens to you, think about what you and your partner can do to grow the relationship together. Think about asking your new partner to discuss and plan things together and find shared goals. Let him know the things that are important to you. Help him to understand your needs, and learn how to ask him to understand your needs. Talk together about growing the friendship between you.

These things will help you and your partner to grow your new relationship.

---

this excitement carry you along　この興奮があなたを押し流す

20. 関係を育てる

**2人の関係を育てるために、話し合いましょう。
あなたが大切に思っていることを、
分かってもらうのです。**

【日本語訳】
　恋が始まったばかりの頃は、人生が急に慌ただしくなり、何もかもが猛スピードで動いているように感じるでしょう。胸が高鳴り、頭が興奮状態になりますが、それはとても良いことです。でも、この興奮のせいで、2人の関係がどこへ向かっているのか、どのように前に進めばいいのかを考えずに、感情に流されやすくなります。

　そうなったとき、2人の関係を育てるために、彼と協力して何ができるかを考えましょう。新しい彼と話し合って一緒に計画を立て、共通のゴールを見つけるよう頼んでみてください。あなたにとって大切なことは何かを彼にも知ってもらいましょう。あなたが何を求めているかを彼に理解してもらえるよう手引きし、理解してもらえるよう頼む方法を学びましょう。2人の間に友情を育むために話し合いましょう。

　そうすることで、あなたと彼は新しい関係を育むことができるでしょう。

21 *Build Trust*

Trust between two people can grow; it can grow as you get to know each other better and as you learn how to talk together about difficult things that happen. Talking through events that have happened which are harder for you to deal with builds trust between people.

It is sometimes natural to try to hide some things from your partner. You might want to **keep things from your partner** that you think might make you look bad or show you to be weak or unable to make choices or plans.

You will lessen your partner's trust if you hide these things from him. Your partner will know either in his mind or in his heart that you are keeping some important things from him and this will take away his trust.

Build trust by being open with your partner about the things that are hard for you to share, as well as the things that are easy to share. Make a habit also of listening to him about the things that are hard for him to deal with.

keep things from your partner パートナーに秘密にしておく

21. 信頼を築く

相手の信用を得るためには、
隠し事をしないことです。
隠しておきたいことこそ、伝えるのです。

【日本語訳】
　人と人との信頼は深まるものです。お互いをよく知り、身の回りで起きた困難な出来事について話し合うことで信頼は深まります。あなたにとって対処するのが難しい出来事が起きたら、そのことについてじっくりと話し合うことで信頼関係が築かれます。
　彼に隠し事をしようとするのは自然なことです。自分の印象を悪くするようなことや、自分の弱さや優柔不断さを露呈するようなことは、彼に秘密にしておきたいと思うものです。
　でも隠し事をすると、彼の信頼を損ねることにつながります。あなたが何か重要な隠し事をしていることを、彼は頭や心で感じ取るでしょう。そうなると、彼の信頼を失うことになります。
　彼に話しやすいことも、隠しておきたいこともオープンに話すことで、信頼を築きましょう。また、彼にとって扱いづらい物事についても、彼の話に耳を傾ける習慣をつけましょう。

22 *Choose Your Feelings*

We have heard women say, 'He made me feel bad' or, 'She made me feel sad.' No one can make you feel anything without your OK. You choose to feel good or bad about what has been said. The other person can't make you feel it, you do. In truth, people feel good or bad because of **what they say to themselves about what another person has said**.

If your partner says, 'I don't like what you are wearing' you can think, 'Well that's **his point of view** but I like it and I am happy with it and I am going to wear it.' Or you can say 'Why does he always hurt me with what he says, he doesn't love me, I look bad, I am not pretty.'

Wow! Two very different ways of thinking about what your partner said. The first one just says he can have that point of view, but you don't share it. The second makes the comment grow into a hurtful unkind view that may not even be true.

It is always what you say to yourself about what the other person has said that hurts the most, not what they really said to you.

---

22. 気持ちを選ぶ

**本当にあなたを傷つけるのは、
人の言葉ではありません。
その言葉を受けたあなた自身が、
自分に投げつける言葉なのです。**

【日本語訳】

　よく女性がこんなことを言っているのを耳にしたことはありませんか？　「彼に嫌なことを言われた」「彼女に悲しいことを言われた」と。でも、誰もあなたの了承なしにあなたに感情を抱かせることはできません。言われたことに対して、良い気持ちになるか悪い気持ちになるかはあなた自身が選択しているのです。相手があなたに感情を抱かせることはできません。あなたがそれを抱くのです。実際、人は相手が言ったことに対して自分にどんな言葉を投げかけるかで、良い気持ちになったり悪い気持ちになったりするのです。

　彼が「君の服装、好きじゃないな」と言ったとしたら、あなたは「それは彼の考え方でしょう。私はこの服が気に入っているし、満足しているから着るわ」と思うこともできますし、「どうして彼はいつもそんなことを言って私を傷つけるの？　彼は私のことを愛していないんだわ。私はブスで可愛くないんだわ」と思うこともできます。

　彼が言った言葉の受け取り方がこんなに違うなんて、すごいですね！　前者は彼がそう思うのは自由だけど、私は共感しないという考え。後者はその一言を、事実とは異なるほど人を傷つける思いやりのない言葉に変えてしまっています。

　本当にあなたを傷つけるのは、相手が実際に言った言葉ではなく、その言葉を受けたあなた自身が自分に投げつける言葉なのです。

23 *Enjoy Yourself*

Remember to enjoy yourself, to have fun, to be light and cheerful, at least most of the time.

There are times when you might not feel happy or times when you have things to worry about. You might have to work hard at times and focus strongly, but it is still possible to be happy and light.

There are many times when you could choose to be lighter and more cheerful. **This will help your spirit**; it will make you stronger and **more able to get along with others** when times are hard for you. Being light and happy makes you more pleasant with your family and friends. Sharing your fun and happiness with your partner can add to the enjoyment of both of you.

You can choose to enjoy yourself more, and to have more fun.

---

this will help your spirit これは精神的な支えになる   more able to get along with others もっと人と仲良くする

23. 自分自身を楽しむ

**どんな時にも、できるだけ明るくいるように
心がけましょう。
そうすることであなたは強くなり、
人との関係もうまくいくようになります。**

【日本語訳】

　できるだけ多くの時間を、明るく楽しく元気よく過ごすよう心がけましょう。

　不満や心配事を抱えているときもあるでしょう。がんばって働かなければならないときや、しっかり集中しなければならないときも。それでも明るくハッピーでいることはできます。

　もっと明るく元気でいられるときはたくさんあります。これは精神的な支えになります。明るく元気でいることで、うまくいかないときも気持ちを強く持って、もっと人と仲良くすることができます。明るくハッピーでいれば、家族や友人とも楽しく過ごせますし、彼と楽しくハッピーな時間を共有することができれば、お互いに楽しみが増えます。

　自分からもっと楽しもうと心がけることで、もっと楽しむことができるのです。

24 *Ask Questions*

Learn to ask questions about your partner. Show a real interest in what he thinks and feels. Don't be afraid to ask.

Some people don't find it easy to ask their boyfriend or partner about themselves. If you are one of these people, make the effort to do this. Ask questions such as, 'What are you feeling now?' or 'What is happening right now for you?' or 'Can I help you with anything?' Then listen to his answer. Really listen. Don't start asking another question or make a comment. Wait and **listen to him with all your heart**.

Learn to proceed quietly and be a loving, listening person. Grow your understanding, grow your friendship, and this will grow your love.

listen to him with all your heart　心をこめて彼の話を聞く

24. 質問する

彼の考えていること、思っていることを
尋ねることを怖がらないで。
そして質問をしたなら、
彼の答えにじっと耳を傾けるのです。

【日本語訳】
　パートナーに彼自身のことを質問できるようになりましょう。
彼の考えや気持ちにすごく関心を持っていることを示しましょ
う。尋ねることを恐れないで。
　恋人やパートナーに彼自身のことを尋ねるのが難しく感じる
人もいます。そういう人は次のような努力をしてみてください。
「今どんな気持ち?」「今あなたの中で何が起きてるの?」「何か
手伝えることはある?」といった質問をしてみましょう。そし
て彼の答えに耳を傾けます。真剣に耳を傾けましょう。途中で
他の質問をしたり、口を挟んだりしてはいけません。最後まで
じっと、心をこめて彼の話を聞きましょう。
　静かに話を進め、思いやりのある聞き上手になりましょう。
理解を深め、友情を育てれば、愛を育むことができます。

25 *Don't Jump Ahead Of Yourself*

Everyone can do so much at a time; we are all able to think about many things at once. **Jumping ahead of what is happening at the moment** happens because you can think about many things at the same time, including thinking about the future. Thinking too much about the future will not support what you are doing right now.

'I am always thinking about tomorrow and when the day is over I feel unhappy because I haven't done much. I think it's because I think too much about tomorrow and not enough about what I am doing right now.'

Lon

Be aware of the present moment; give it your best, rather than going too far forward. Be aware and enjoy the present moment.

---

jumping ahead of what is happening at the moment 今この瞬間に起こっていることよりも、先のことを考える   be aware of the present moment 今この瞬間に目を向ける

25. 先のことを考えすぎない

将来のことを考えすぎるのはやめましょう。
大切なのは今この瞬間です。

【日本語訳】

　誰でも一度にたくさんのことをやりすぎることがあります。私たちは皆、一度にいろんなことを考えることができるからです。今この瞬間に起こっていることよりも、先のことを考えてしまうのは、同時にたくさんのことを考えることができるからです。例えば、未来のことなど。先のことを考えすぎても、今やっていることの助けにはなりません。

　「私はいつも明日のことを考えていて、その日の成果が少ないと、一日の終わりに不満を感じます。明日のことを考えすぎて、今やっていることに意識が十分に向けられていないからだと思います」　　　　　　　　　　　　　　　　　　　　　　　　ロン

　今この瞬間に目を向けましょう。ずっと先の未来ではなく、今この瞬間に全力を注ぎましょう。そして、今を意識して存分に楽しみましょう。

26 *Be Yourself In Your Relationship*

Sometimes people try to act like something or someone they are not. Don't try to pretend that you are like another person. That is hard to keep up and **you do yourself harm by trying**.

Keep explaining your values, your thoughts to your partner. Your values and thoughts are very important as they become who you are.

You don't have to agree with the other person's values and thoughts to have a happy relationship. But you need to express your values and beliefs to give the other person the chance to understand who and what you are, even if they don't agree with you. You also need to think about how you can accept their values even if you don't agree with them.

---

you do yourself harm by trying　そうしようとすることであなた自身が傷つく

26. 彼の前でもあなたらしく

別人であるかのようにふるまってはいけません。
相手に本当のあなたを分かってもらい、
あなたらしくいることこそが大切なのです。

【日本語訳】
　人はときどき、自分ではない誰かになろうとすることがあります。別人であるかのようにふるまうのはやめましょう。別人のふりを続けるのは困難ですし、そうしようとすることであなた自身が傷つくからです。
　あなたの価値観や考えを彼に説明し続けましょう。あなたの価値観や考えはとても大切です。それらはいずれあなたがどんな人かを表すものになるからです。
　幸せな関係を築くために、相手の価値観や考えに同意する必要はありません。あなた自身の価値観や考えを相手に説明して、あなたがどんな人かを理解してもらう機会を作りましょう。たとえ相手があなたに同意しなくても構いません。あなた自身も、相手に同意しない場合でも相手の価値観を受け入れる方法を考えましょう。

SECTION

4

KEEPING THE FLAME OF LOVE ALIVE AND HEALTHY

愛の炎を絶やさず健全に保つ

'There is no remedy for love but to love more.'
Henry David Thoreau

「愛の治療薬はもっと愛することしかない」

ヘンリー・デイヴィッド・ソロー

27 *Forgiveness*

Everyone finds it hard to forgive someone who has done something that hurts you or something thoughtless. It is easy to **go on thinking** much too often about what it was they did to hurt you.

Doing so does not help you to **get on with your life**. It does not help you to live your life in a happy way. The other person might have hurt you once; but when you think about it over and over again, you hurt yourself again and again. Every time you think about it you **relive the hurt**. By reliving the pain in your mind over and over again, do you not hurt yourself more often than the other person **hurt you in the first place**?

Learn to forgive other people when you think they have hurt you or done something wrong to you. Also, learn to forgive yourself for things you have done wrong or could have done better.

The past is gone and finished. If you have done something wrong, learn from what you have done and try never to do it again. Forgive yourself and think about how you can be better in the future.

go on thinking　考え続ける　　get on with your life　前向きに生きる　　relive
the hurt　痛みを思い出す　　hurt you in the first place　あなたを傷つけたそもそも
の原因

27. 許す

あなたを傷つけた人を許すのは難しいことです。
でも、その出来事を考え続けることが、
さらにあなたを傷つけていることに
気づきましょう。

【日本語訳】
　誰にとっても、自分を傷つけるようなことや思いやりのないことをした相手を許すことは、難しいものです。ともすれば、あなたを傷つけた相手の言動が何だったのか、考え続けてしまいます。

　ずっと考えていても前向きに生きる助けにはなりません。幸せに生きる助けにはならないのです。相手があなたを傷つけたのは一度かもしれませんが、そのことを何度も思い出して考え続けると、あなたは自分自身を何度も傷つけることになります。そのことを思い出すたびに痛みを思い出すからです。頭の中で痛みを何度も思い出すことによって、相手があなたを傷つけたそもそもの原因よりも頻繁にあなた自身を傷つけることにはなりませんか？

　誰かに傷つけられたり、間違ったことをされたと思ったときは、相手を許すことを学びましょう。同時に、あなた自身が間違ったことをしたり、もっとうまくやれば良かったと思うときにも、あなた自身を許すことを学びましょう。

　過去はもう過ぎたことです。間違ったことをしたら、そこから学び、二度と同じ過ちを繰り返さないようにすれば良いのです。あなた自身を許し、将来どうすればもっと良くなるかを考えましょう。

28 *Goals With Regard To Your Partner's Parents And Family*

Having a relationship with one special person does not mean that the relationship is with that one person alone. They may have parents, brothers and sisters and other family. It is unusual to have a relationship without contact with your partner's family.

Keep in your mind that your partner's family has had a long relationship with him. They will know each other well and will have ways of talking with each other and doing things with each other. Remember also that they have their own ways to show their love for each other.

Do not feel strange or alone when you are with his family. Sometimes you may even think that they don't want you in their lives or the life of their son. Remember that they love him and want what they feel will be the best for him.

Try to understand them. Listen to them carefully and ask them questions so you may **come to know them better**. Do not feel that you need to own your partner and keep him apart from his family; show that you are happy to share him with his family.

keep in your mind　心に留めておく　　come to know them better　彼らのことを
もっと知る

28. 私と彼と彼の家族

彼を独り占めしようとしないこと。
彼の家族のことを知る努力をしましょう。

【日本語訳】

　交際は、その相手との関係だけを意味するものではありません。彼には両親がいて、兄弟姉妹、親戚もいるかもしれません。相手の家族と接点を持たない交際はまれです。

　彼の家族は彼と長年のつき合いであることを心に留めておきましょう。彼らはお互いをよく知っていて、彼らなりの話し方や物事のやり方があります。愛情の示し方も彼らなりの方法を持っていることを覚えておきましょう。

　彼の家族と一緒にいるときに違和感や孤独を感じないようにしましょう。ときには彼らがあなたを邪魔者扱いしているとさえ感じることもあるかもしれません。彼らは彼を愛していて、彼にとってベストだと彼らが思うものを望んでいる、ということを忘れないようにしましょう。

　彼の家族のことを理解する努力をしましょう。彼らの言葉にじっくりと耳を傾け、彼らのことをもっと知るために質問をしてみましょう。彼を独り占めしようとしたり、家族から遠ざけようとしたりしないこと。彼のことを彼の家族と喜んで共有する姿勢を示しましょう。

29 *Goals For Happiness*

Most people want to be happy in their lives. They want to be happy in their relationship, their work, their friendships and in the way they learn.

It can be too easy to think that having lots of money or lots of things will bring happiness. Most people who have lots of money or many things say that these do not bring happiness. They say that to have many things or lots of money leads them to worry about keeping their money or their things, more than enjoying them.

Think carefully about **what you would like to achieve in your life**—what you think would help you to be happy. Having some money and some things is important for you and it is valuable to have goals about these things.

Think about other parts of your life. Is good health important to you? Is a loving relationship important to you? Is it important to you to have some time to yourself every day? Do you have something you love to do? Do you read, paint, swim, dance, walk or enjoy doing something else?

Making goals for these things will help you to enjoy a balanced, happy life.

what you would like to achieve in your life 人生であなたが成し遂げたいこと

29. 幸せのゴール

お金や物があっても、
幸せになれるとは限りません。
人生で本当に成し遂げたいことは何かを
真剣に考えてみましょう。

【日本語訳】

　人はたいてい、幸せな人生を送りたいと望んでいます。恋も仕事も友情も、そして勉強も順調であることを望んでいます。

　お金や物をたくさん持っていれば幸せになれると思いがちですが、お金や物をたくさん持っている人のほとんどが、たくさんあっても幸せにはなれないと言います。彼らが言うには、物やお金をたくさん持っていると、それ自体を楽しむことよりも、それらを維持する悩みのほうが大きいそうです。

　人生であなたが成し遂げたいことは何かをじっくりと考えましょう。あなたを幸せにするのものは何なのか。お金や物をある程度持っていることは大切ですが、これらの物事の目標を設定しておくことが非常に重要です。

　人生のお金や物以外の部分について考えてみましょう。健康はあなたにとって重要ですか？　恋愛関係はどうですか？　毎日自分の時間を持つことはあなたにとって重要ですか？　趣味はありますか？　読書、絵を描くこと、水泳、ダンス、ウォーキングはしますか？　その他の楽しみはありますか？

　これらの物事の目標を設定しておくと、バランスの取れた幸せな人生を送ることができます。

30 *Show Compassion*

Compassion is showing care and kindness to another person rather than being hard or distant and judging others in a hard way. It shows that you have a kind heart. Compassion for another person is finding the strength to care about them even when they have done something wrong, bad, or hurtful without thinking of you or of others.

Compassion guides you to listen to the other person and discuss their problems. Listening and really hearing can help you to understand them and to think kindly of them. Don't try to help them to find an answer to their problem; only they can do that. Listening with your heart open is **the valuable thing** to do for them and for you.

Compassion is also about being kind to yourself as well as being kind to the other person.

---

show compassion　思いやりを示す　　the valuable thing　有益なこと

30. 思いやりの心を示す

思いやりの心というのは、
相手のことを考えられる強さのことです。
そしてそれは、自分自身のことも
大切にするということです。

【日本語訳】
　思いやりとは、人にやさしく親切な態度を示すことです。他人に冷ややかな態度を取ったり、他人を厳しく判断したりするのは思いやりではありません。思いやりはあなたが親切な心を持っている証です。人に思いやりの心を持つことは、誰かがあなたや他人のことを考えずに何か間違ったことや悪いこと、人を傷つけるようなことをした場合でさえも、相手のことを気にかけてあげる強さを持つことです。

　思いやりは相手の話に耳を傾け、相手の問題について話し合うようあなたを導いてくれます。耳を傾け、真剣に聞くことで相手を理解し、相手のことをやさしく思いやることができるのです。でも、答えを見つける手助けをしてはいけません。それができるのは本人だけです。心を開いて相手の言葉に耳を傾けることは相手にとってもあなたにとっても有益なことです。

　思いやりは人に対しても自分に対してもやさしくすることなのです。

31 *Keep Alive A Strong Vision For Your Love*

Very often love starts out being exciting, fresh, new, fun and it can sometimes go on like this. It can be far too easy to **take the other person's love for granted**. If this happens, there is a risk that the love loses its energy and the relationship loses its hope for the future.

There are lots of ways to keep your love strong and healthy for the future and one of these is to keep alive a strong vision for your love. **A vision or picture of the future** as you would like it to be, of you and your partner.

Showing your love and friendship and enjoying each other is an example of a good vision for the future.

Share your vision with your partner. Talk with him about how he feels about your vision. Ask him if he shares this vision. Keep your vision fresh and alive.

---

take the other person's love for granted　愛されているのを当然と思う
a vision or picture of the future　思い描いた未来

31. 恋の未来を思い描く

**情熱を保ち続ける方法の1つは、
将来の夢を彼と語り合うことです。**

【日本語訳】
　恋は最初はワクワクして新鮮で楽しいものですが、しばらく
経つと相手の愛情に慣れて、愛されているのが当然と思ってし
まいがち。そうなってしまうと、愛はエネルギーを失い、2人
の関係から未来への希望が失われる危険性があります。
　未来のために愛を強く健全な状態に保つにはさまざまな方法
がありますが、その1つがしっかりとしたビジョンを持ち続け
ることです。あなたが望む2人の未来を描きましょう。
　愛と友情を示し、2人でいることを楽しんでいる未来は、良
いビジョンの一例です。
　あなたのビジョンを彼と分かち合いましょう。あなたのビジョ
ンについて彼がどう思うか話し合い、同じ未来を彼も思い描い
ているかどうか尋ねてみましょう。そのビジョンを新鮮に保ち
ましょう。

32 *Make Love The Goal*

Goals are important in any relationship. The best way to build your love together is to have positive goals, things you want or will do, rather than negative goals, things you don't want or want to stop doing.

Take time to **connect with your partner** and the love between you and make some goals together, such as how you are going to talk with each other, how much time you want to spend together, how you are going to grow the friendship between you, how you are going to show your love for each other.

Focus on what you want rather than what you don't want. Have some very clear goals about the love you want because this **helps your mind to stay clear and focused**. Your mind is always looking forward to a goal that is positive rather than a negative goal. Be careful to show your love as your number one goal.

connect with your partner　パートナーと心を通わせる　　helps your mind to
stay clear and focused　頭をクリアにして集中した状態に保つ

32. 恋愛にも目標を

あなたがこうありたいと思う愛の形について、
よりはっきりとした目標を持ちましょう。

【日本語訳】
　どのような関係にも目標を持つことは大切です。共に愛を育む最善の方法は、ポジティブな目標（あなたが求めることや、やりたいこと）を持つこと。ネガティブな目標（あなたが求めないことや、やめたいこと）は避けましょう。

　時間をかけてパートナーと心を通わせ、愛を育み、一緒に目標を立てましょう。例えば、お互いに相手にどのような話し方をするか、どのくらいの時間を一緒に過ごしたいか、どうやって2人の間に友情を育むか、どのようにお互いへの愛情を示すかなど。

　あなたが求めないことではなく、求めることに注目しましょう。あなたが求める恋愛について、明確な目標をいくつか持ちましょう。これにより頭をクリアにして集中した状態に保つことができるからです。あなたの頭は常に、ネガティブな目標よりもポジティブな目標を求めているものです。一番の目標として愛情を示すことを心がけましょう。

33 *80% Positive*

It is sometimes very easy to talk too much about the things that have gone wrong for you or have not been pleasant for you. If you speak mostly about all the negative things in your life or relationship, that is **how you will be seen by others**. It also is **how you will come to believe yourself to be**.

The things that have gone wrong for you are probably only a small part of what you have done. Most of the things you do are OK and you might feel happy about them. The things that have gone wrong in any day are probably less than 20% of what you have done in that day.

Make sure that you talk positively about the things that are OK for you or are good in the world. Make sure that what you talk about is at least 80% positive and less than 20% negative. You will feel happier and the world will seem a better place.

how you will be seen by others　あなたが他の人にどのように見られるか　　how you will come to believe yourself to be　自分がそのような人だと信じるようになる

33. 80% ポジティブ

ネガティブなことばかり話してはいませんか。
会話の80%は
ポジティブな内容にしていきましょう。

【日本語訳】
　人は自分にとってうまくいかなかったことや不快だったことばかり話してしまいがち。人生や恋愛についてネガティブなことばかり話していると、あなたが他人にそう見られてしまいます。そしてあなたも、自分がそのような人だと信じるようになってしまうのです。

　あなたにとってうまくいかなかったことは、あなたがやったことのほんの一部のはずです。それ以外はたいていうまくいっていて、あなたはそれに満足しているでしょう。うまくいかなかったことは、一日の中でおそらく、あなたがその日に行ったことの20% もないはずです。

　あなたにとってうまくいったことや世の中の良い出来事についてポジティブに話すことを心がけましょう。少なくとも会話の80%はポジティブな内容にして、ネガティブな内容は20% までに抑えましょう。そうすることで、あなたもハッピーな気分になり、世界がより良い場所に見えてきます。

34 *Tell The Truth*

In a relationship it is important to **be honest with each other**, to tell the truth. If you don't tell the truth, your partner might see this as something wrong with the relationship. He might think you have something that is worrying you. He might think you don't trust him with your feelings, or that you are **keeping something from him**.

Let's say he asks you, 'Am I working too many long hours? Do you need me to spend more time with you?' You might think of saying, 'No, it's fine. Everything is OK'. He knows that he is never at home; he knows the hours he works are long. So if you don't tell him the truth, next time he asks you about something, he may question **whether you are trying to be nice to him** and whether he can trust your answer.

If you do not tell the truth, you might think that you are being kind to your partner, but you really are not being fair to him or to yourself. Tell the truth with kindness, but tell the truth.

---

be honest with each other　お互いに正直である　　keeping something from him　彼に何か隠し事をする　　whether you are trying to be nice to him　彼に気を遣っているのかどうか

34. 本音を話す

本音を話すことはとても大切です。
相手に遠慮してばかりではいけません。
あなたが本当に思っていることを伝えるのです。

【日本語訳】
　恋愛関係においては、お互いに正直に本音を話すことが大切です。本音を話さないと、彼は2人の関係が何かおかしいと感じるかもしれません。彼はあなたに何か気がかりなことがあるのかと思ってしまうでしょう。彼のことを心から信用していないと思うかもしれないし、あなたが彼に何か隠し事をしていると思ってしまうかもしれません。

　彼にこう聞かれたとしましょう。「僕は長時間働きすぎかな？君との時間をもっと作って欲しい？」。あなたはこう答えようとします。「ううん、大丈夫よ。何も問題ないわ」。彼は自分が家にいないこと、長時間働いていることを知っています。ですから、あなたが本音を話さなければ、次に彼があなたに何かを尋ねるとき、彼はあなたが彼に気を遣っているのか、あなたの答えを信じていいのか分からなくなるでしょう。

　本音を話さないと、あなたは彼にやさしくしているつもりでも、実際には彼に対してもあなた自身に対しても公平ではないのです。やさしい口調で本音を話し、あなたが本当に思っていることを伝えましょう。

35 *Ask For The Truth*

Sometimes your partner will say things to you to be nice or pleasant to you, rather than being 100% truthful.

You might be in a dress shop and you really like a dress. Let's say your partner is good at picking dresses that **look good on you**, and you ask him whether one suits you. He knows that this dress is not for you, perhaps the line just isn't right for your body or the color is wrong. If he's truthful he will say that it doesn't look exactly right for you. If he tries to please you, he might say that it looks good on you rather than tell you the truth.

Which would you rather hear?

Make it clear to your partner that you want him to be truthful with you every time, even if he thinks that **what he says may not be what you would like to hear**. Promise not to react badly if he tells you something you don't like.

---

look good on you あなたに似合う　　what he says may not be what you
would like to hear 彼の言葉があなたの聞きたい言葉と違っているかもしれない

35. 本音を尋ねる

彼にも本音で話してもらいましょう。
たとえあなたの望む答えではなくても、
怒ったりしてはいけません。

【日本語訳】

　彼が100%本音で話さず、やさしい言葉や嬉しい言葉をかけてくれることもあるでしょう。

　洋服屋に行って気に入ったドレスがあったとします。彼はあなたに似合うドレスを選ぶのが上手で、あなたは彼に、そのドレスが似合うかどうか尋ねたとします。このドレスはラインがあなたの体型に合っていなかったり、色が合ってなかったりして、彼はあなたに似合わないと思っています。彼が本音を話していたら、あなたにあまり似合わないと言うでしょう。あなたを喜ばせようとしていたら、本音を言わずに、似合っていると答えるかもしれません。

　どちらの答えをあなたは聞きたいですか？

　たとえ彼の言葉があなたの聞きたい言葉と違っていたとしても、常に本音で話してほしいと彼にはっきりと伝えておきましょう。それがあなたの気に入らない答えであっても、怒ったりしないと約束しましょう。

36 *Let Go Of Control*

Most people do not like being told what to do. When you tell someone what to do you may be trying to control them rather than wanting the best for them.

Controlling another person's actions and thoughts by trying to get them to act or think differently will not be successful **in the long term**. When one person tries to control the other, this makes a problem in the relationship. One person will be unhappy that **the other person will not do what they ask** and the other person will be unhappy that they are not trusted to make good choices.

Ask for the things you need in a relationship without trying to control what the other person says or does. This way, if the person does what you ask, they do it because they are free to do it, not because you are trying to control their actions and thoughts.

It is not possible to control another person; if you try, you will make them and yourself very unhappy.

---

in the long term 長期的には   the other person will not do what they ask
自分の頼んだことを相手がしてくれない

36. コントロールしない

人は命令されるのが嫌いです。
相手をコントロールしようとしても、
それは決して成功しないどころか、
2人の関係を危うくします。

【日本語訳】
　人はたいてい命令されるのが嫌いです。誰かに命令をすると
き、あなたはその人に最善のことを望んでいるのではなく、相
手をコントロールしようとしているのかもしれません。
　誰かの行動や考えを変えさせようとして、その人の行動や考
えをコントロールすることは、長期的にはうまくいきません。
片方が相手をコントロールしようとすると、2人の関係に問題
が生じます。片方は自分の頼んだことを相手がしてくれないこ
とに不満を持ち、もう片方は自分の判断を信用してもらえてい
ないことに不満を持ちます。
　相手の言動をコントロールしようとせずに、2人の関係に必
要なものを求めましょう。そうすれば、相手が自分の頼んだこ
とをしてくれた場合でも、あなたが相手の行動や思考をコント
ロールしようとしたからではなく、相手が自らの選択でそれを
したことになります。
　他人をコントロールすることは不可能です。そうしようとす
ることで、相手も自分も不満に感じてしまうのです。

37 *Learn From Each Other*

Throughout your life you will learn and go on learning. **Everything you do gives you a chance to learn** more about yourself. Being in a relationship is a great way to learn about yourself because when you are close to another person you notice things about them and you that are worth thinking about.

You will always learn from each other in relationships. You will notice things that happen and think about your feelings about these things. You may think about what you could do better next time and if you are brave enough, **you can change the way you do things for the better**.

This is how you learn from another person; by noticing your feelings and then changing the way you do things.

everything you do gives you a chance to learn あなたの行いのすべてが自分について学ぶ機会となる　you can change the way you do things for the better 物事のやり方を改善する

37. 互いに学び合う

人とつき合うということは、
自分を知るよいチャンスです。
相手から学び、
よりよい方法を学ぶこともできるのです。

【日本語訳】

　生涯を通して人は学び続けます。あなたの行いのすべてが自分について学ぶ機会を与えてくれます。恋愛は自分のことを学ぶとても良い機会です。人と深くつき合うと、相手と自分についての気づきがあり、そのことについて考える貴重な機会が得られるからです。

　恋愛を通して人はお互いから常に何かを学びます。何かが起きたことに気づき、そのことについて自分がどう思うか考えます。次はどうすればもっとうまくいくのかを考え、あなたにその勇気があれば、物事のやり方を改善することもできるでしょう。

　こうして人は人から学びます。自分の気持ちに気づいて、物事のやり方を変えることによって何かを学ぶのです。

38 *Look For Happiness*

Everyone has a sense of happiness in them, of being able to look on the bright side of things. In your life, things that happen can sometimes be hard for you. You will have some good times and some difficult times, some good days and bad days.

When things are difficult for **some of the time** you will need to think about fixing whatever has caused the problem. You may think about what you can do differently or better next time.

At the same time you can choose not to over-worry about the problem; doing so can be a waste of your energy. Be lighter in your spirit during difficult times, both in your actions and your relationships. Choose not to think about the problems all the time, think about the happy things in your life and **be grateful for these happy things**.

You can choose to look for the happiness even when things are difficult.

---

some of the time しばらく   be grateful for these happy things 幸せな出来
事に感謝する

38. 幸せを探す

常に何かに悩んでいると、
生きるエネルギーが損なわれてしまいます。
人生のよい面を思い、そのことに感謝しましょう。

【日本語訳】
　誰もが、物事の良い面を見ることができる、幸せの感覚を持っています。人生にはつらい出来事が起こることもあります。良いときもあれば悪いときもあり、良い日もあれば悪い日もあります。
　つらい時期がしばらく続いたら、問題の原因が何であっても、それを修正する方法を考える必要があるでしょう。そんなときは、次回はどうすれば良いかを考えると良いでしょう。
　同時に、問題について心配しすぎるのも良くありません。エネルギーの無駄になる場合があるからです。行動面でも恋愛関係においても、つらい時期には心を軽くしましょう。いつまでも問題について考えるのはやめて、人生の良い面について考え、幸せな出来事に感謝しましょう。
　つらいときでも幸せを探すことはできるのです。

39 *Do Nice Things For Your Partner*

Remember to do nice things for your partner. Something thoughtful or pleasant will be thought of very kindly by your partner and will help the relationship to be healthy and grow.

When you do something pleasant you are showing that you love your partner and that you care so much for them that you wish to please them in small or big ways. Mostly, a small gift or act will be enough; **it does not need to cost a lot of money**. It is the thought that is important, the thought that shows your love.

Give your partner a small written note, or a card with a message of love, a book or a letter or some small thing that he likes. This will tell him how much you care for him. These are all small things that do not cost a lot of money but which show how much you love him.

Do nice things for your partner often.

---

it does not need to cost a lot of money　たくさんお金をかける必要はない

39. 彼の喜ぶことをする

もっと彼を喜ばせましょう。
お金をかける必要はありません。
あなたが彼を喜ばせようとすることが、
彼の心を動かすのです。

【日本語訳】

　彼の喜ぶことをするよう心がけましょう。思いやりのあること や喜んでもらえることをすると、彼にとても親切に思われ、 2人の関係を健全に保ち、育むのに役立ちます。

　喜ばれることをすると、彼に対するあなたの愛と、あなたが どれだけ彼を大切に思っているかが伝わります。彼を少しでも 喜ばせたいと思っていることが伝わるからです。ほとんどの場 合、ちょっとしたギフトや行動で十分です。たくさんお金をか ける必要はありません。大切なのは思いです。愛を伝えるのは 思いだからです。

　彼にちょっとしたメモや愛のメッセージを書いたカードを贈 りましょう。本や手紙、彼が好きなちょっとした物でも構いま せん。彼にあなたの思いを伝えるにはそれで十分なのです。こ れらは、お金をかけずに彼への愛の大きさを伝えるちょっとし た方法です。

　彼の喜ぶことを頻繁にするよう心がけましょう。

40 *Touch Your Partner Often*

One of the things that babies and children value very much is the sense of touch. Being touched is important to them and to **their sense of well-being** and safety. As you grow up, this wonderful part of your life—touching, and being touched—may not happen as much. Somehow we get the idea it's not OK for grown-up people to touch so much.

Touch your partner often. A gentle touch on the arm or a soft touch to the face is friendly; it talks to both of you about your love and helps your well-being. Hold hands. Sit close when watching TV or when you are both sitting reading together. You may not be aware of how much a gentle touch can help you build your love for each other. **Your heart will recognize this touch** and it will add to building a loving relationship.

---

their sense of well-being　幸福感　　your heart will recognize this touch　あなたの心はこの触れ合いを感じる

40. スキンシップ

触れ合うことはとても大切です。
スキンシップは2人の愛を大きく育てます。

【日本語訳】
　赤ちゃんや子供が重視することの1つに、肌が触れ合う感触
があります。子供たちにとってスキンシップは、幸福感と安心
感を与えてくれる大切なものです。スキンシップは人生の素晴
らしい一部ですが、大人になるにつれてその頻度は減ってしま
います。なぜか大人はあまりスキンシップを取るべきではない
という考えになるからです。
　彼と頻繁にスキンシップを取りましょう。腕にやさしく触れ
たり、親しみをもって顔にそっと触れたりすると、2人の愛を
確認することができ、幸福感が生まれます。手をつなぎましょ
う。テレビを見るときや一緒に座って読書をするときには、そ
ばに座りましょう。あなたは気づいていないかもしれませんが、
やさしく触れることでお互いの愛がもっと深まります。あなた
の心はこの触れ合いを感じ、愛し合う2人の関係がさらに深ま
るのです。

41 *Listen Carefully Before You Speak*

Your mind can bring up thoughts and pictures much faster than you can speak words. This is one reason that you might find it hard to listen fully when another person is talking. Your mind can easily move to other thoughts while the other person is speaking. Your mind can start to think about what you will have for lunch or what you will do when you get back to work.

It is very easy for you to **start to think ahead** while another person is speaking. It is easy to think of what you might say next after the other person has finished talking and it is **your turn to speak**.

Thinking too far ahead shows a lack of respect for the other person. Listen carefully and seek to understand the other person and it will show care that honors them. **The other person can sense** if you are not listening carefully. When you listen with care it helps to make a close and positive relationship.

Take special care to listen to your partner.

---

start to think ahead 次のことを考え始める   your turn to speak 自分が話す
番   the other person can sense 相手は気づくものだ

41. 話す前によく聞く

相手の話をちゃんと聞くことは、
難しいものです。
だからこそ相手の話を注意深く聞く態度が、
相手への気持ちを示すことになるのです。

【日本語訳】
　　脳は言葉を話すよりもずっと速く、考えや映像を映し出すことができます。これは、人が話している間、集中して聞くのが難しい理由の1つです。相手が話している間、思考が簡単に逸れてしまうからです。お昼は何にしようかなとか、仕事に戻ったら何をしようかなとか考え始めてしまうでしょう。

　　相手が話している間、次のことを考え始めるのはよくあることです。相手が話し終えて自分が話す番が来たら何を言おうか、などと考えてしまうのです。

　　ずっと先のことを考えていると、相手に敬意のない態度が表れてしまいます。相手の話を注意深く聞き、理解しようとすることで、相手に対する敬意を示すことができます。あなたが注意深く聞いているかどうか、相手は気づくものです。相手の話にしっかりと耳を傾けることで、2人の関係が親密でポジティブなのものになります。

　　彼の話には特に耳を傾けるよう心がけましょう。

42 *Be Friends As Well As Lovers*

Love is the base for a successful relationship and friendship is the food that helps the relationship to grow and be healthy. This is a good balance; friendship and love together strengthen a relationship and help it to stay healthy and strong.

Love comes from a deep sense of togetherness and joining of the spirit or soul. Love is mostly about your feelings, **whereas friendship is very much about how you both get along together**. Long term success in a relationship **needs friendship as well as love**. Learning about the other person builds the friendship. You can grow the friendship by listening, being thoughtful, being helpful, being kind and caring.

Remember to keep friendship as a real part of your relationship, as well as love.

---

whereas friendship is very much about how you both get along together
友情は 2 人の仲によるところが大きい   needs friendship as well as love 愛情と
同じく友情が必要

42. 恋人であり同時に友人である

2人がよりよい関係を保つためには、
愛情と同じく友情が必要です。
この2つのバランスがよければ、
2人の関係はより強固なものになるのです。

【日本語訳】
　　愛は良い関係の基盤であり、友情は関係を育み、健全に保つ
ための糧となります。愛情と友情のバランスが良ければ、2人
の関係は強まり、健全でしっかりとした状態を保つことができ
ます。
　　愛情は深い一体感と心のつながりから生まれます。愛はお互
いの気持ちによるところが大きいですが、友情は2人の仲によ
るところが大きいです。良い関係を長く続けるには、愛情と同
じく友情が必要です。友情は、相手のことをよく知ることで育
むことができます。相手の話に耳を傾け、思いやりを持ち、相
手を助け、親切に接すれば友情が深まります。
　　2人の関係に愛情と同じく友情を維持するよう心がけましょ
う。

43 *Listen To Your Inner Wisdom About Love*

When things aren't working in your relationship and it doesn't feel right, listen to your inner wisdom. Here are some ideas:

- Breathe deeply and listen to what's happening inside of you.

- Ask yourself, 'What is the best thing for me to do about this right now?' Let go and wait for an idea or thought to come. It might take minutes or days, but an answer will come.

- **Be alert** and look for answers around you; you may just feel a small understanding of what to do next.

- You may be talking with someone and they will say something that answers your question.

- Act upon this small understanding, do what you believe needs to be done.

Your inner wisdom often knows things that your thinking does not see or know.

Trust yourself because **no matter what advice you get from other people**, it is you that has to deal with your life and your relationships.

---

listen to your inner wisdom あなたの内なる声に耳を傾ける be alert アンテナ
を張る no matter what advice you get from other people 人からどんなアド
バイスをもらったとしても

43. 内なる声に耳を傾ける

うまくいかないとき、
何かがおかしいと感じるときには、
あなたの内なる賢明さに、
静かに耳を傾けましょう。

【日本語訳】

　2人の関係がうまくいっていなくて、何かがおかしいと感じたら、あなたの内なる声に耳を傾けましょう。アイデアをいくつかご紹介します。

- 深呼吸をして、心の中で何が起こっているか、内なる声に耳を傾ける。

- 「このことについて今、自分にできる最善のことは何か？」と自分自身に問いかける。アイデアや考えが浮かぶのを待つ。時間はかかったとしても答えは必ず出ます。

- アンテナを張って身の回りで答えを探す。次に何をすればいいかちょっとした気づきがあるかもしれません。

- 人と話す。話しているうちに、相手の言葉の中に答えが見つかるかもしれません。

- このちょっとした気づきを行動に移す。自分が信じることをやりましょう。

　思考だけでは見えないことや分からないことを、多くの場合、あなたの内なる声は知っています。

　自分自身を信じましょう。人からどんなアドバイスをもらったとしても、あなたの人生や2人の関係を何とかするのは自分なのですから。

44 *Look For Things You Really Like About Each Other*

It is easy to be hurt by small things that your partner does. Thinking too much about these things can make you very unhappy. If you are not careful, bad feelings about small things can **come to be what you think about most of the time**.

Don't spend too much time thinking about all the small things that are bad about your partner. Balance this by thinking about what you really like and love about him. There will be much more that you like than you dislike.

Right now, think about three things that he does that are kind or are nice for you.

Learn to balance the small bad things with the good things he does. Learn to accept the small things because that is what they are... small things.

come to be what you think about most of the time　あなたの思考の大半を占める

44. 長所を見つける

**彼の些細な欠点を気にかけてばかりいませんか。
今すぐ、彼のいいところを3つ挙げてみましょう。
そして欠点とのバランスを考えてみるのです。**

【日本語訳】
　女性は彼の些細な行動に傷つきやすいもの。些細なことを気にしすぎると、大きな不満につながることも。気をつけないと、些細なことに対する嫌な気持ちがあなたの思考の大半を占めてしまいます。
　彼の欠点ばかり考えるのに時間を使うのはやめましょう。欠点と彼の好きなところをバランスよく考えましょう。嫌いなところよりも好きなところのほうが多いはずです。
　あなたに対して親切なところ、やさしいところを3つ挙げてみてください。
　些細な欠点と彼のいいところとのバランスを取ることを学びましょう。些細なことを受け入れることを学びましょう。所詮それらは、些細なことですから。

45 *Have Loving Thoughts About Each Other*

Do you remember the dreams and passion you had at the start of your relationship? Do you believe that you should have this love always? Sometimes it is not as easy to feel this kind of love **on a day-to-day basis**. Everyday living sometimes puts to one side your dream of a great love.

Remind yourself daily to be loving and gentle with your partner so you can link yourself and him with your dream of love. Having loving thoughts about the other person helps you to be more loving and kind and is a healthy way to live your life.

When you think mostly of the good and positive things about your love you make it easier to accept and not worry about the small things you do not like.

loving thoughts　愛情あふれる思いやりの心　　on a day-to-day basis　日常の中で

45. 思いやりを持つ

恋愛が始まった頃の情熱を維持するのは
難しいものです。
毎日の生活の中で、
愛情あふれる思いやりの心を相手に示しましょう。
それがあなたを愛ある生活へと導きます。

【日本語訳】
　つき合い始めた頃に思い描いた夢や、感じた情熱を覚えていますか？　この愛がずっと続くと信じていますか？　日常の中でこのような愛を感じるのが難しいときもあるでしょう。日々の生活に追われて、素晴らしい恋愛の夢を脇に追いやってしまうからです。

　毎日、彼に思いやりを持ってやさしく接することを心がけましょう。恋愛の夢と2人をリンクすることができるように。相手に思いやりの心を持つと、愛を持ってやさしく接することができ、健やかに過ごすことができます。

　恋愛について良いことやポジティブなことばかり考えていると、気に入らない些細なことでも受け入れやすく、気にならなくなります。

46 *Keep A Clear Picture Of Your Love*

Keep a clear picture in your mind of the love you feel for your partner. **Imagine what you like about them** in your mind, think about what their strengths are and the things you love them to do and say. Keep this picture even if it is not in your life right now. Have this clear picture of what you want in your future relationship as this helps to make it happen.

Love and happiness are usually part of that picture. Dream about your future with as much love and happiness as you can. Expect the best from your relationship and believe that **it can come true for you**.

---

imagine what you like about them　彼の好きなところを思い浮かべる　　it can come true for you　あなたにとって現実となる

46. 理想をはっきりと思い描く

あなたが手にしたいと思う理想の愛の形を、
はっきりと思い浮かべましょう。
それが、理想を現実のものにする助けとなります。

【日本語訳】
　彼に対して感じる愛情をはっきりと思い描きましょう。心の
中で彼の好きなところを思い浮かべ、彼の長所は何か、彼にし
てほしいこと、言ってほしいことは何かを考えましょう。今、
恋をしていなくてもこのイメージを持ち続けましょう。将来の
恋愛に求めることを、はっきりとイメージしておきましょう。
そうすることで、実現に近づきます。
　愛と幸せは、たいていその理想の一部です。愛と幸せに満ち
た未来を夢見ましょう。最高の恋愛を期待し、それが現実にな
ると信じるのです。

47 *Accept Differing Ideas And Beliefs*

Do you and your partner have different ideas and beliefs? If you do then you are **like most people** in relationships. It is common in relationships to have beliefs and thoughts that are different from your partner.

It is easy to **get caught up with the thoughts and beliefs that you do not share** rather than with all the thoughts and beliefs that you do share—there are probably more of the latter than you think.

Accept that the differences between people add to the pleasure and richness of life. This is especially important in a relationship.

Look at the ideas and beliefs that you share and build on these. This way the relationship can grow and become stronger and this can lead to a healthy love.

---

like most people 多くの人と同じように　　get caught up with the thoughts and beliefs that you do not share 自分とは違った考え方や価値観にとらわれる

47. 違いを受け入れる

誰でも違った考え方や価値観を持っています。
その違いにとらわれすぎてはいけません。
違いを受け入れることは、
2人にとって重要なことです。

【日本語訳】
　　あなたと彼は違った考えや価値観を持っていますか？　もし
そうならば、交際中の多くの人たちと同じです。価値観や考え
の違う相手とつき合うことはよくあることです。

　　考えや価値観の違いにばかりとらわれて、考えや価値観が近
い部分を見逃しがちですが、意外と共通点のほうが多いもので
す。

　　人との違いが、人生に喜びや豊かさを添えることを受け入れ
ましょう。これは恋愛において特に重要です。

　　考えや価値観の共通点に目を向けて、共通点を増やしましょ
う。そうすることで、2人の関係が深く強固なものとなり、健
全な愛へとつながるのです。

48 *Balance The Way You Talk*

For a relationship to work, the way you talk to the other person needs to be mostly positive. Think and talk about positive things you see in them. If you keep telling them all the things they don't do well, it will break down the love between you and **the relationship can fall apart**.

Saying the same negative things over and over to your partner does not build a happy relationship.

Build a happy relationship by talking most of the time about the things that are working well; only talk about the things that are not working in a way that is kind and helpful. Take care to balance the way you talk with your partner.

the relationship can fall apart　2人の関係が壊れる可能性がある　　saying the same negative things over and over to your partner　ネガティブなことを彼に言い続けること

48. 話し方に要注意

**相手にはポジティブに語りかけるように
しましょう。**

【日本語訳】
　恋愛でうまくいくには、相手への話し方を常にポジティブな
ものにする必要があります。相手の良い面に目を向けて、それ
を伝えるようにしましょう。相手の悪い面にばかり目を向けて
指摘し続けると、2人の愛に亀裂が生まれ、関係が壊れる可能
性があります。

　ネガティブなことを彼に言い続けると、幸せな関係は生まれ
ません。

　うまくいっていることについて話すようにすることで、幸せ
な関係を築きましょう。うまくいっていないことを話すときは、
やさしく相手のためになるような方法で。彼と話すときはバラ
ンスに気をつけましょう。

49 *Love Can Be All That You Hope For*

All relationships need work and care to develop and grow. Love can be for you all that you hope but remember that love never stays the same, it changes all the time. Sometime it feels better, sometimes it feels like it isn't working. **As time goes by,** love will feel different as it grows and changes.

Have goals for your relationship and work with your partner to gain these. Practice the things needed to grow your love, such as talking and listening and showing your love for each other. You and your partner can live through these times, grow together and learn to love each other more and more as time passes.

---

as time goes by　時間が経つにつれて

49. 愛は望みどおりに

2人の関係は、ともに育てていくことが必要です。
愛はいつも同じではありません。
ときとともに変化していくものです。

【日本語訳】
　2人の関係を発展させ育てるには、努力と愛情が必要です。あなたが求めるのは愛情だけかもしれませんが、愛はいつも同じではなく、常に変化していくものだということを忘れないで。うまくいっているように感じるときもあれば、そうでないときもあります。時間が経つにつれて愛情の感じ方も違ってくるでしょう。愛は育ち、変化するものだからです。
　2人の関係にゴールを設け、彼と協力して達成する努力をしましょう。愛を育てるために必要なことをしましょう（会話すること、相手の話を聞くこと、お互いの愛を示すこと、など）。2人は愛の変化を乗り越え、共に成長し、お互いをもっと愛することを学ぶでしょう。

SECTION
5
THROUGHOUT IT ALL
どんなときでも

'A successful marriage requires falling in love many times, always with the same person.'
Mignon McLaughlin

「幸せな結婚には、
何度も同じ相手に恋に落ちることが必要です」

ミニョン・マクラフリン

50 *Learn From Everything*

Happy and positive events in your life make your soul strong and happy; negative and difficult events allow you to think about the way to do things and how you could do them differently next time. Negative and difficult events can also make your soul stronger.

You learn the most from events that are the most difficult for you. You learn the least from those that are least difficult.

When things happen to you that are positive or happy, you will enjoy them but do you think about them? Do you think about what caused them or have led them to you? Do you **think through** what you might learn from those events?

When things happen that make you unhappy or negative, you have an important choice. You can either be angry or you can think about what you might learn from them and how you might act differently in future.

think through　じっくりと考える

50. すべてのことから学びを得る

**人は困難から、より多くを学ぶものです。
不幸な出来事にただ怒りをあらわにするか、
そこから何かを学ぼうとするか。
あなたはどちらを選びますか。**

【日本語訳】
　幸せでポジティブな出来事は心を強く幸せにしてくれます。ネガティブで困難な出来事は、次はどうすればいいのかを考えるきっかけを与えてくれます。また、ネガティブで困難な出来事は心を強くしてくれます。

　人は困難から多くを学ぶもの。困難が小さいと学びも少なくなります。

　ポジティブで幸せな出来事が起こったら、それを喜ぶだけではなく、その出来事について考えることはありますか？　それが起こった原因は何か、なぜそうなったのか。その出来事から何を学べるかじっくりと考えることはありますか？

　不幸やネガティブな事が起こると、人は重要な選択を迫られます。怒りをあらわにするか、それともそこから何かを学び、次はどうすればいいか考えるか。あなたはどちらを選びますか？

51   *Move Past Anger*

Everyone has events that happen to them that can leave them feeling **angry and upset**.

For example, **if you are treated badly at work** and you feel that you have done a good job, you have a choice. You might feel that it is not fair and dislike whoever has treated you badly and be angry. You might **feel like a victim** and ask yourself why the world is not kind to you, and feel angry. Or you might try to understand that sometimes things happen that are not nice, that whatever happened is past, is over and you should move on with your life.

There is no value in staying angry in your mind. Move on and be pleased with yourself for being positive. The choice is to be strong and learn, or to be sad and **pity yourself**. You make that choice.

angry and upset 怒りやとまどい   if you are treated badly at work もし職場で不当な扱いを受けたら   feel like a victim 被害者になりきる   pity yourself 自分を憐れむ

51. 過去の怒りを忘れる

よくないこともときには起こります。
ですがそれは過去のこと。終わったことなのです。
いつまでも怒りにとらわれたりせず、
前に進むことです。

【日本語訳】
　怒りやとまどいを感じる出来事は誰にでも起こります。
　例えば、自分では良い仕事をしたと思っていたのに、職場で不当な扱いを受けたとしたら、あなたには選択肢があります。不公平だと言って不当な扱いをした相手を嫌い、怒りをあらわにするか。被害者になりきって世界はひどい場所だと嘆き、怒りを抱くか。あるいは、こういうこともあると割り切って、終わったことだと前を向くか。
　怒りを持ち続けることに価値はありません。前を向いてポジティブな自分を喜びましょう。強く学ぶ姿勢でいるか、悲嘆に暮れて自分を憐れむか、あなたはどちらを選びますか？

52   *Teach Each Other*

A loving relationship gives many great chances for two people who are close friends to understand each other better, and to understand themselves better. The reason for this is the amount of friendship and trust that can be created between two people in a close relationship. Trust may start with love but will grow with friendship and **sharing**. In sharing, there are times when you can learn new things about yourself as well as your partner.

New experiences give plenty of chances to learn and grow in your skills and knowledge. When you have a close relationship, you can help each other to understand the things that happen to you and **what lessons you might learn**. A close relationship gives you safety where you can learn.

With your partner, agree that you can talk to each other about your experiences and share in learning about what happens to each of you.

---

sharing 思いの共有   what lessons you might learn そこから得られる教訓

52. 互いに教え合う

相手への信頼は愛から生まれるかもしれませんが、それを育てるのは友情と共有する思いです。

【日本語訳】
　恋愛は、2人の親しい友人の間に、お互いそして自分自身への理解を深める素晴らしい機会を与えてくれます。親密な2人の間には、大きな友情と信頼が生まれるからです。恋から始まった信頼関係だとしても、それを育てるのは友情と思いの共有です。思いを共有することで、自分自身についても相手についても新たな気づきを得ることがあります。

　新しい経験は、スキルや知識の学びと成長のチャンスをたくさん与えてくれます。親しい関係にあると、周りで起こるさまざまな出来事やそこから得られる教訓について、お互いに理解を促すことができます。親しい関係は、安心して学べる環境を与えてくれるのです。

　彼と協力して、それぞれが経験したことについて話し合い、そこから得られる学びを共有するようにしましょう。

53 *Dealing With Difficult Times*

All relationships have difficulties at times. Sometimes difficulties mean that love is over and **the relationship is really at an end**. Other times difficulties will give you a chance to think carefully about what you want and whether your love is worth making changes to allow the relationship, and both of you, to grow.

If you feel unhappy in your relationship, think with some care about this question. Do you think and feel that you and your partner might be able to talk through each other's needs? Can you talk with each other, or does **your talking always lead to fights**? Can you try to work through differences?

If you can, then be prepared to listen as well as talk about your needs. Be prepared for change, but also be prepared for you and your partner to do things differently together and to work toward happiness again.

---

dealing with difficult times　困難な時期に立ち向かう　　the relationship is
really at an end　2人の関係が本当に破綻してしまう　　your talking always lead
to fights　話し合いはいつもけんかに発展する

53. 困難な時期に立ち向かう

２人の間に生じた問題は、
関係を変化させるチャンスかもしれません。
そして２人を成長させるきっかけに
なるかもしれません。

【日本語訳】
　交際がうまくいかない時期は誰にでもあります。それが恋の
終わりを意味し、２人の関係が本当に破綻してしまうことも。
一方で、困難な時期は、あなたが何を求めていて、何かを変え
てまでこの関係を発展させる価値がお互いにとってあるかどう
かを、じっくりと考える機会を与えてくれます。
　２人の関係に不満があるのなら、以下の点について注意深く
考えてみましょう。あなたと彼は、お互いのニーズについてじっ
くりと話し合うことができますか？　２人で話し合うことはで
きますか——それとも話し合いはいつもケンカに発展してしま
いますか？　お互いの違いを受け入れる努力はできますか？
　もし答えが「できる」なら、自分のニーズについて話し、相
手の言葉にも耳を傾ける準備をしましょう。変化に備え、これ
までとは違ったアプローチで幸せに向けて再び努力する準備を
しましょう。

54 *Moving Forward*

When difficult times come up in a relationship it can be easy to either blame yourself for being the cause of the problem, or blame your partner. The truth is that one person alone is never responsible for a problem between two people; mostly, problems arise with each person **playing some part in making the problem**.

When there's a problem, first try to think of what part you have played in creating it. Be truthful but don't overstate your part. **If you blame yourself for everything** you will be too hard on yourself and take away from your **self-esteem**.

If you blame your partner for all of the problems in the relationship you will take away any chance of you both talking through the problem.

Be prepared to accept that you have probably added to whatever difficulties you are having in your relationship and accept that you can talk with your partner about these difficulties as a step **along the path to growing together**.

playing some part in making the problem　起きた問題にいくらかの責任がある
if you blame yourself for everything　すべてを自分のせいにするなら
self-esteem　自尊心　　along the path to growing together　ともに成長する道
を歩む

54. 前に進む

問題が起こったとき、
原因はどちらか一方にあるのではなく、
何らかの形で両方にあるものです。
自分を責めすぎるのも、相手を責めすぎるのも、
間違いです。

【日本語訳】
　2人の関係がうまくいかないときは、問題の原因を作った自分や相手を責めがちです。しかし本来、2人の間に起きた問題について、どちらか片方だけの責任ということはあり得ません。問題が起こったとき、それぞれにいくらかの責任があるものです。

　問題が起こったら、自分がどのような原因を作ったかをまず考えてみましょう。正直に、でも自分の責任を誇張するのはやめましょう。すべてを自分のせいにすると、自分自身に厳しくなりすぎて自尊心を奪ってしまいます。

　2人の間に起きた問題のすべてを彼のせいにすると、2人でじっくりと話し合って問題を解決するチャンスを失います。

　2人の間に起きた問題について、自分にも非があったかもしれないことを認め、ともに成長する道を歩むための一歩として、彼とそのことについて話し合う心の準備をしましょう。

55 *Don't Hold Back Your Love*

Women have **an inbuilt gift** for caring and showing love, but some women hold back their love when they feel that their love and friendship are not returned the way they would like. If their boyfriend or partner is not showing his love in the way they want, they feel forgotten and unhappy. If this continues, **these feelings can take over** and turn into dislike and anger.

It is important to love openly and **not close down your love**, even if you feel you are not receiving the love you want. Talk with your partner about how you feel and explain how you would like to be treated. This shows care for yourself and the long-term relationship.

---

hold back your love 気持ちを抑える　　an inbuilt gift 天賦の才能　　these feelings can take over そういった気持ちが心を占めて　　not close down your love 愛することをやめない

55. 気持ちを抑え込まない

あなたの思ったように愛情や友情が
示されなかったとしても、
あなたの気持ちを抑え込んではいけません。
愛することをやめてはいけません。

【日本語訳】
　女性は思いやりや愛情を表現する天賦の才能を持っています。
ところが、思ったように愛情や友情を返してもらえないと、気
持ちを抑え込む女性もいます。ボーイフレンドやパートナーが、
自分が思ったような愛情を示してくれないと、忘れられたよう
に感じて不満を抱きます。これが続くと、そういった気持ちが
心を占めて嫌悪感や怒りに変わってしまいます。
　思ったように愛情が受けられなかったとしても、愛すること
をやめずに愛情をオープンにすることが大切です。あなたの気
持ちを彼に伝え、どのように扱ってほしいかを説明しましょう。
これにより、あなたが自分を大切にし、長期的な関係を望んで
いることが相手に伝わります。

56 *Trying To Please Everyone Doesn't Work*

Everyone is busy in their work and women can **find it hard to please everyone** in their lives. Doing your work well, having a happy relationship, relaxing and spending time with friends and family are hard to do all at once. Sometimes all this can lead to stress.

You cannot please everyone. It is best to have some very clear thoughts about what you want for yourself and follow these, rather than trying to be all things to everyone and trying to make everyone happy. Remember to listen to your own beliefs and values and follow these. **Work out what you believe in** and follow that every day. If you do this you will be less stressed and a happier, more honest person.

---

find it hard to please everyone　すべての人を満足させるのは難しいと感じる
work out what you believe in　あなたが何を信じるかをよく考える

56. 皆を喜ばせようとしない

**すべての人を満足させることなどできません。
あなたにとって本当に必要な人は誰なのか、
心の声に耳を傾けるのです。**

57 No-one Stays The Same

It's easy to think that your partner will stay the same as he was when you first met. Change always happens in every relationship, at different times and **at different stages of the relationship**. Adapting to change is something you need to do as the relationship grows. **Adapting to change** means being able to see the changes that are happening around you and keeping an open mind to doing things differently.

Relationships usually start with lots of things that you both like about each other. It's easy to forget why you liked each other at first when things change in your life. Every day, try to remember the good things about the other person and tell them about these things.

This helps to **look after the relationship in a very special way**.

at different stages of the relationship　恋愛のステージ　adapting to change
変化に順応する　look after the relationship in a very special way　2人の関係
をすごく大切にする

57. 人は変わるもの

変わらない人などいません。変化していくことは
2人の関係を成長させる上で
とても大切なことなのです。

【日本語訳】
　女性は、彼が出会った頃のままでいてくれるものと思いがち。
ですが、恋愛は時とともに常に変化するものであり、恋愛のス
テージによっても変わっていきます。恋愛関係の発展とともに、
あなたも変化に順応する必要があります。変化に順応するとは、
あなたの周りで起きている変化に気づき、それを受け入れ、自
分自身の行動を変えることを意味します。
　恋愛はたいてい、お互いの好きなところをたくさん見つける
ところから始まります。ところが、人生に変化が起きると、そ
もそも相手のどこを好きになったのか忘れてしまうことも。毎
日、相手のいいところを思い出すよう心がけましょう。そして、
それを相手にも伝えましょう。
　そうすることで、2人の関係をすごく大切にすることができ
ます。

58 *Stay Connected To Your Feelings*

Throughout your relationship stay connected to your feelings. Take notice and think about your feelings without being hurt or upset.

Your feelings will always help you to understand what is happening in your world and in your relationship. They are very useful in telling you if something is or isn't right. They can connect you to what is happening for you and what is happening around you.

Sit gently with these feelings and carefully listen to them. Sometimes you will decide to act upon them, sometimes you will just notice them and feel kindness to yourself for feeling them and then let them go.

stay connected to your feelings 自分の心の声に常に耳を傾ける

58. 自分の心の声に常に耳を傾ける

自分の気持ちにもっと耳を傾けましょう。
そしてその心の声に従うのです。
心の声は、あなたに警告を与えてくれたり、
状況を的確に判断してくれたりするものです。

【日本語訳】

　恋愛中は自分の心の声に常に耳を傾けましょう。傷ついたりとまどったりするのではなく、自分の気持ちに気づき、大切にしましょう。

　あなたの気持ちは、あなたの周りや2人の関係に起きていることへの理解を常に助けてくれます。何かがうまくいっているかどうかを、あなたに教えてくれます。あなた自身やあなたの周りで何が起きているかを、あなたに知らせてくれるのです。

　自分の気持ちに向き合って、静かにじっと耳を傾けましょう。気持ちに従って行動をしようと思うこともあれば、そんな気持ちを抱いている自分をいたわり、気持ちを解放することもあるでしょう。

59 *When You Decide To Act On Your Feelings*

When you decide that you want to do something about how you feel, ask questions about what you think is happening and check with your partner about how you can go forward together with a better understanding of each other.

But always remember to **be true to yourself**. Act on what is true for you and on what you believe is right for you. Be yourself and act calmly and clearly with your partner. Expressing your values can help you to be more in control and less emotional.

'It doesn't work for me in my relationship if I lose who I am and don't notice my values, because I then **end up hating** the other person because I am not who I really am with them.'

Mary

Be true to yourself always.

---

be true to yourself 自分に正直でいる   end up hating 結局は嫌いになる

59. 気持ちに正直に

自分に正直でいましょう。
自分の価値観をしっかり持っていれば、
感情的でない落ち着いた行動が
とれるようになるはずです。

【日本語訳】
　あなたの気持ちをどうにかしたいと思ったら、何が起きているかを自分自身に問いかけてみましょう。そして、彼と2人で、お互いをもっと理解して前に進む方法について確認し合いましょう。

　でも、常に自分に正直でいること。あなたの気持ちに正直に、あなたが正しいと思うことをしましょう。自分らしくふるまい、彼に冷静にはっきりと対応しましょう。あなたの価値観を伝えることで、感情的にならずにうまくコントロールできるようになります。

　「私の場合、自分らしさを見失って自分の価値観に気づかないと、恋愛はうまくいきません。なぜなら、一緒にいるときに本当の自分でいられないと、相手のことを結局は嫌いになってしまうからです」
　　　　　　　　　　　　　　　　　　　　　　　　メアリー
　常に自分に正直でいましょう。

60 *When You Think Too Much*

Sally is a woman who worries too much. She said, 'I really worry about small things that happen. Sometimes these things have happened three days ago and I am still worrying about them. If my boyfriend does something that I don't like, I worry about it endlessly.'

Sally makes small thing into big things often. Something small becomes something big because she has thought too much about it for three days.

Do you think too much about the past and then that becomes a worry? Are you an **over-worrier**? Some people think about something that happened yesterday and this turns to worry about what they said or didn't say, or could have said to their partner.

The key is to let go of thoughts about the past and live in present time. Just **remind yourself what you are doing now**. You may be sitting in a chair or in a train or at work or sitting at home; wherever you are right now is important. Try to bring yourself back to what is happening at this moment.

Thinking about the past and trying to change something that has already passed is a very hard way to treat yourself. No one can change the past. **Let go of what you said or did yesterday** and look at where and what you are doing right now.

---

over-worrier 心配性の人　remind yourself what you are doing now 今自分がしていることを自分自身にリマインドする　let go of what you said or did yesterday 昨日言ってしまったことや、やってしまったことは忘れる

60. 考えすぎてしまうとき

誰であっても過去を変えることはできません。
過去について思い悩んでも、何も解決されません。
それよりも大切なのは、あなたの「今」です。
今を生きることを考えるのです。

【日本語訳】

　サリーは心配性です。彼女はこう言います。「ほんの些細なことでもすごく心配してしまうんです。3日前に起きたことでさえ、いまだに考えてしまいます。彼が嫌なことをしたりしたら、いつまでも思い悩んでしまいます」。

　サリーはよく、小さなことを大げさに捉えてしまいます。3日間も考えすぎたせいで、小さなことが大きなことになってしまうこともしばしば。

　過去のことを考えすぎて、そのことが悩み事になってしまうことはありますか？　あなたは心配症ですか？　昨日起こったことを考え続けて、彼に言ったこと、言わなかったこと、あるいは言ったかもしれないことについて心配してしまう人もいます。

　過去のことを考えるのをやめて、今を生きることが大切です。今、自分が何をしているかを自分自身にリマインドしましょう。椅子に座っているかもしれないし、電車に乗っているかもしれないし、職場かもしれないし、自宅かもしれませんが、とにかく今あなたがやっていることが大切なのです。今この瞬間に起きていることに意識を戻すよう心がけましょう。

　過去のことを考えて、過ぎてしまったことを変えようとするのは、自分にひどい扱いをしているも同然です。誰も過去を変えることなどできません。昨日言ってしまったことや、やってしまったことはもう忘れて、今あなたがどこで何をしているかに意識を向けましょう。

Don't Try To Change The Other Person

Many people start a relationship thinking they can fix someone else or make another person better in a way they want them to be. This does not work. Don't ever believe that asking someone to change will make them change; it won't. If someone else is ready to change, they will change because they want to, not because someone else has asked them to do it.

People do not change because you ask them to. People change because their life is such that they have to change because what they are doing is so **uncomfortable** or hurtful to them that they have to find a better way to do it.

Love and accept your partner. Change the things about yourself you can change and love and **accept them as they are**.

---

uncomfortable 不快な   accept them as they are あるがままの相手を受け入れる

61. 相手を変えようとしない

相手を変えようという試みは、
決して成功しません。
相手を変えようとするのではなく、
あるがままの彼を愛せるように、
自分を変えるのです。

【日本語訳】
　　相手の悪いところを直してあげたり、自分が望むような人に
変えられると信じて交際を始める人がいます。でも実際にはそ
うはいきません。変わってほしいと頼めば相手が変わってくれ
ると信じてはダメ。そうはならないからです。人が変わるときは、
本人がそうしたいからであり、誰かに頼まれたからではないの
です。
　　人は誰かに頼まれたからといって変わるものではありません。
人が変わるのは本人が自分から変わらなければならないと思う
ような状況に陥り、今の状況が自分にとってすごく不快だった
りつらかったりするために、より良い方法を求めて変わろうと
するのです。
　　彼を愛し、受け入れましょう。自分自身の変えられる部分を
変えて、ありのままの相手を愛し、受け入れるのです。

62 Don't Put Others Before Yourself

Do you **care for yourself** well, or do you see the other person's needs as more important than your own? When you care for yourself and begin from strength you will have more energy to care for another person in a relationship. Caring for yourself well is strength, not weakness.

Just because you could do so much for another person doesn't mean you should. You must keep some energy for yourself. Sometimes caring for yourself means saying 'No' to someone you love.

'Your first love needs to be of self. Without that you have very little to give.'

Jenny

---

put others before yourself 自分よりも他人を優先する   care for yourself 自分を大切にする

62. 人を自分より優先しない

自分を大切にすることは、
弱さのあらわれではありません。
自分を愛することができて初めて、
他人を思いやることができるのです。

【日本語訳】
　あなたは自分を大切にしていますか？　それとも自分自身が求めていることよりも、相手が求めていることの方が大事だと考えていますか？　自分を大切にして力がみなぎっていると、恋愛においても相手のことを大切にするエネルギーが生まれます。自分を大切にすることは強さであり、弱さではありません。
　相手のためにもっとできることがあったとしても、必ずしもそれをすべきではありません。自分のためにエネルギーを残しておきましょう。ときには自分を大切にするために、愛する人の要求を断ることも必要です。
　「最初に愛するべきは自分なのです。自分を愛せなければ他人を思いやる余裕もなくなります」　　　　　　　　　ジェニー

63 *Have Energy For Yourself*

Living a busy life and having so many different areas of your life that need your time can **break down your energy**. If you feel like your energy is getting low, here are some things you can do to keep good strong energy for yourself:

- Find time to be by yourself, for yourself.

- Say, 'No' if you have too much to do.

- Ask for help if and when you need it.

- Make a list of all the good things about yourself and read it every day for a month.

- Work out something you enjoy doing and make time to do it every day, even if just for half an hour.

- Have more sleep or relaxation.

Any of these things will help you to keep strong positive energy for yourself.

---

break down your energy あなたのエネルギーを損なう

63. 自分のためのエネルギー

毎日忙しくしていると、
エネルギーが切れてしまうことがあります。
そんなときには、積極的に充電する時間や
機会を持ちましょう。

【日本語訳】
　忙しい日々を送り、さまざまな用事を抱えていると、時間を奪われ、エネルギーが損なわれてしまいます。エネルギーが低下していると感じたら、良いエネルギーをしっかりと保つために以下のことを試してみましょう。

- 自分のための一人の時間を作る
- 用事をたくさん抱えているときは断る
- 必要なときは助けを求める
- 自分自身の長所をリストアップして、1ヵ月間毎日読む
- 楽しめることを見つけて、たとえ30分でも毎日それをやるための時間を確保する
- 睡眠やリラックスの時間を増やす

　上記のいずれも、強くポジティブなエネルギーを維持するのに有効です。

64 *Distance Yourself From Friends You Cannot Trust*

If you feel that a friend is not true or honest with you or does not share your values, talk with them first and try to **clear things up between you**. If they continue to be **dishonest and not supportive of your values**, you can make the decision not to spend time with them. You can do this quietly without making trouble.

If you hold on to a friendship when you cannot trust that friend, you are likely to **bring harm and pain to yourself**. You may think that you should accept them as they are and give them another chance, but to do so will **lessen your self-esteem** and can invite trouble and hard times to you.

If they are being dishonest or your trust and friendship is not returned, your spirit will feel that the relationship is not fair to you. Your self-esteem will be lessened. Your friendship with others who are truer to you may also be lessened.

You need to distance yourself from others who are not trustworthy.

---

clear things up between you 互いの間の問題を解決する　　dishonest and not supportive of your values 誠意がなく、あなたの価値観を支持しない　　bring harm and pain to yourself あなたに悪影響と苦痛をもたらす　　lessen your self-esteem あなたの自尊心を損なう

64. 信用できない友人と距離をとる

**友人があなたにとって信用できない態度を
取り続けるなら、
勇気を持って距離を置くことです。
つき合い続けると、
あなた自身がすり減ってしまいます。**

【日本語訳】
　友人があなたに正直に本音で話していない、またはあなたの価値観に共感していないと感じたら、まずは話し合ってお互いの間の問題を解決しようと努めましょう。それでも誠意がなく、あなたの価値観を支持しない態度を取り続けるなら、一緒にいるのをやめるという決断を下すのもあり。その場合は、トラブルにならないようにそっと離れましょう。

　信用できない友人と友人関係を続けると、あなたに悪影響と苦痛をもたらす可能性が高いです。ありのままの彼らを受け入れ、もう一度チャンスをあげようと思うかもしれませんが、そうすることによりあなたの自尊心が損なわれ、トラブルや困難を招く可能性があります。

　相手が信用できない態度を取り、あなたの信頼や友情に報いてくれないのならば、あなたの心はこの関係が公平ではないと感じるでしょう。あなたの自尊心も損なわれてしまいます。あなたにとって信用できる友人との友情さえも傷つけてしまいかねません。

　信用する価値のない相手とは距離を置きましょう。

65 *Be Careful How People Talk To You*

Have you ever walked away from a friend and felt badly? Felt like something the other person did or said wasn't nice or didn't feel right? Sometimes friendships change and **your friends may not have your best interests at heart**. They may feel jealous of what you have.

Trust that feeling of something not being right if you feel it about a friend. Sometimes you have to **let go of a past friendship** because it is not healthy for you anymore.

'I loved my school friend Sak, but she was so jealous of my life with my boyfriend and my job. We just didn't have any fun together. I miss her but I had to stop seeing her as it was poisoning my life. It was just not nice to be with her any more, she was becoming so **cruel**.'

Lucy

---

your friends may not have your best interests at heart 友人は、本当はあなたのためを思っていないかもしれない   let go of a past friendship 過去の友情を手放す   cruel 残酷な

65. 友人が言うことに注意する

友情も変化することがあります。
もし友人があなたのことを思っていないと
分かったなら、
勇気を持って、過去の友情を手放しましょう。

【日本語訳】
　　友人と距離を置いて嫌な気持ちになったことはありますか？
相手の言動がひどいと思ったり、何かおかしいと思ったことは？
友情は変わることもありますし、友人は、本当はあなたのため
を思っていないかもしれません。あなたが持っているものに嫉
妬しているかもしれません。
　　友人と一緒にいて何かがおかしいと感じたら、その気持ちを
信じましょう。健全な友情ではなくなっているときは、過去の
友情を手放すこともときには必要です。
　　「私は、学生時代からの友人であるサックのことが大好きだっ
たんですが、彼女は、私の彼氏や仕事にすごく嫉妬していました。
一緒にいても全然楽しくなかったです。彼女と離れて寂しいけ
れど、私の人生に害をもたらしていたので会うことを断念しな
ければなりませんでした。彼女と一緒にいても居心地良くなく
なっていたし、彼女はすごく残酷な人になってしまいましたか
ら」
　　　　　　　　　　　　　　　　　　　　　　　　　　ルーシー

SECTION
6
WHEN LOVE IS OVER
愛が終わったら

'If you love something, set it free;
if it comes back it's yours,
if it doesn't, it never was.'
Richard Bach

「何かを愛したら、それを手放しましょう。
戻ってきたらそれはあなたのもの。戻ってこなかったら、
最初からあなたのものではなかったのです」

リチャード・バック

66 *Freedom Of Choice*

There may come a time when you feel you have done everything you can in a relationship and it just does not seem to be working.

If you have put the time and effort into your relationship and done everything you can to make it work, if your partner does not want to change and if you are always unhappy, you have three choices.

1. You can choose to change your thoughts about what you want from your partner and the relationship.

2. You can accept who and what your partner is.

3. You can **leave the relationship**.

If you are worried about your relationship, give careful thought to these three choices.

---

leave the relationship つき合いを解消する

66. 選択の自由

あらゆる努力をしても、
2人の関係がうまくいかなくなったとしたら、
じっくりと考えることが必要です。

【日本語訳】

　2人の関係のためにできることはすべてやったのに、それで
もうまくいかないと感じる時期もあるでしょう。

　時間と労力を費やして、関係改善のためにあらゆる努力をし
たけれど、彼は変わりたがらず、あなたがいつも不満を感じて
いるなら、あなたが取れる選択肢は3つです。

- 彼や2人の関係に求めることに対する、あなた自身の考え
  を変える
- ありのままの彼を受け入れる
- つき合いを解消する

　2人の関係に悩んでいるなら、上記の3つの選択肢について
じっくりと考えてみましょう。

Know When To Leave

In a new relationship, everyone hopes that their love will grow and that both of you will become stronger together, happily growing as a loving couple. This doesn't always happen.

While many relationships do grow, some do not. This is sad, but true. How do you know when a relationship is over? Your heart will tell you and **your intuition will tell you**. You may feel sad, the pleasure of seeing your partner may go, you may feel doubt and pain and you may feel that the love between you is over.

If you feel these feelings, think very carefully about whether you should stay in the relationship or end it. If you stay in an unhappy relationship, you do not look after your best interests. Long-lasting sadness will hurt you and make it hard for you to be happy again in the future.

If your partner is not able to talk with you honestly about the problems and difficulties that you are feeling, you should take care of yourself and end the relationship.

Know when to leave. Work out how to tell your partner it's over and make your plans to leave.

---

your intuition will tell you   直感が教えてくれる

67. 去り際を知る

不幸な関係を続けていると、
あなた自身が傷つくだけでなく、
将来の幸せをも見失うことになってしまいます。

【日本語訳】

つき合い始めたばかりの頃は、誰もがこの恋が発展し、愛し合うカップルとして強く幸せな関係を築きたいと望むものです。しかし、必ずしもそうなるとは限りません。

多くの恋愛は発展しますが、そうでない場合もあります。それは悲しいけれど現実です。恋愛が終わりを迎えたことはどうすれば分かるでしょうか。あなたの心と直感が教えてくれます。悲しい気持ちになり、彼に会える喜びが消え、疑いや苦痛を感じ、2人の愛が終わったと感じるかもしれません。

こうした気持ちを感じたら、2人の関係を続けるべきか終わりにするべきかじっくりと考えましょう。不幸な関係を続けていると、あなた自身のためにはなりません。悲しみが続くと、あなた自身が傷つき、将来、再び幸せになることが難しくなります。

彼が、あなたが感じている問題や悩みについて正直に話せないなら、あなた自身を大切にして関係を絶つべきです。

去り際を知りましょう。彼にどうやって終わりを告げるかを考え、別れる計画を立てましょう。

68 *Stop Blaming*

Many people blame and judge the person they have loved for all the bad things that have happened in their lives. They do not stop to think that they have added something to these events in some way.

Everyone has more control of their lives than they think they have. It can be very healing to accept that your thoughts and actions may have made your life what it is right now.

Don't blame the person you love or have loved in the past for what has or hasn't worked for you in your life. Accept the things you and the other person have done in the past and **move on**. Don't think over and over about the past.

Fix the things you are able to fix and **let go of the past**. Make changes for the future by the way you think and act now. This will create the best possible future for you and your partner and your life will become much more positive.

stop blaming 責めるのをやめる　　move on 前に進む　　let go of the past 過去を手放す

68. 責めるのをやめる

今も愛している人や、かつて愛した人を
責めるのはやめましょう。
過去を手放し、
未来に向けて気持ちを切り替えるのです。

【日本語訳】
　自分の人生に何か悪いことが起きると、自分が愛した人を責め、悪者だと決めつける人がたくさんいます。立ち止まって、自分にも何かしらの非があったとは考えません。

　人は自分が思っている以上に自分の人生をコントロールする力を持っているものです。今の人生は、自分の考えや行動の結果だということを受け入れると、とても心が癒やされるでしょう。

　何かうまくいかないことがあっても、あなたが愛している人や、かつて愛した人を責めるのはやめましょう。過去にあなたや相手がしたことを受け入れ、前に進みましょう。過去のことを何度も思い出して考えるのはやめましょう。

　直せることは直して、過去を手放しましょう。将来のために、今のあなたの考えや行動を変えましょう。そうすることで、あなたと彼にとって最高の未来を創ることができ、人生ははるかに前向きなものとなるのです。

69 *When Things Are Finally Over*

When a relationship is over and you accept that **it cannot be brought back to life**, there is pain, often there is blame, and sometimes a woman will blame herself for not doing enough to keep the relationship **in good health**.

Time will heal this pain.

If you are blaming your former partner for the failure of the relationship, the sooner you let go of this blame the better it will be for you. Blame is never useful; it does nothing except keep the pain of what went wrong alive in you.

Everyone could find things they could have done better, so forgive yourself for not being better or different in the past and decide to be better in the future. Learn from your mistakes; mistakes help you to make better decisions next time.

As quickly as you are able, put your past relationship behind you. Think about your future and how you are looking forward to the new and exciting things that will come into your life.

---

it cannot be brought back to life 元に戻すことはできない　　in good health
良い状態に

69. 本当に終わってしまったら

もう自分を責めるのはやめましょう。
もっとうまくできたはずだと思うなら、
その経験を未来に生かすのです。

【日本語訳】

　2人の関係が終わり、もう元に戻すことはできないと悟ったとき、胸が痛み、誰かを責めたりしてしまいがち。なかには、良い関係を維持するために自分の努力が足りなかったと自分を責める女性もいます。

　この痛みは時が癒してくれます。

　2人の関係がうまくいかなかったことについて、過去の彼を責めているなら、なるべく早くそれをやめるほうがあなたにとって良いでしょう。人を責めるのが役立つことなどありません。終わってしまった恋愛の痛みを引きずるだけです。

　もっとうまくできたはずのことを見つけることは誰でもできますが、それができなかった自分を許しましょう。失敗から学びましょう。失敗は次にもっと良い判断を下すのに役立ちます。

　できるだけ早く過去の恋愛を忘れましょう。未来のことを考え、これから起こる新しくワクワクするような出来事に目を向けましょう。

70 *The Steps Of Grief*

When a relationship is over, don't be surprised if you feel it quite deeply. When you experience loss in a relationship it is easy to **get lost in grief and pain**. There are five stages of grief and it is sometimes hard to move from one stage to the other.

Denial: 'This can't be happening to me,' not yet crying or letting go, not accepting what has happened.

Anger: 'Why me?' feelings of wanting to fight back or hurt the other person, blaming them for leaving you.

Making a deal: Trying to make deals with the person who is leaving or God, to stop or change what has happened.

Sadness: **An overwhelming feeling of loss**, hurt, feeling sorry for yourself. Feeling lack of control, sad and hopeless.

Acceptance: Accepting the loss of the relationship. Finding the good that can come out of the pain of loss, your goals turn toward the future and you remember the past with fond memories of the other person.

Being aware of where you are on this journey helps in moving forward. You won't feel what you are feeling now forever.

---

get lost in grief and pain 悲しみと苦しみで自分を見失う　making a deal 取引
をする　an overwhelming feeling of loss どうしようもない喪失感

70. 悲しみの段階

悲しみは、「否定、怒り、取引、悲しみ、受容」
という5つのステップを踏みます。
自分が今どの段階にあるか考えてみましょう。
悲しみは、永遠に続くものではないのです。

【日本語訳】

　失恋をすると、驚くほど深い悲しみに包まれるものです。失恋を経験すると、その悲しみと苦しみで自分を見失いがちです。悲しみには5つのステージがあり、1つのステージから別のステージへと進むのが難しいこともあります。

　否定：「まさかそんなはずはない」と、自分に起こったことを受け入れられず、まだ泣くことも忘れることもできない。

　怒り：「どうして私なの？」と、ふられたことについて相手を責めたり傷つけたいという気持ちになる。

　取引：あなたをふろうとしている相手または神様と取引をして、彼を引き止めたり事実を変えようとする。

　悲しみ：どうしようもない喪失感や痛み、悲しみにさいなまれる。自制心を失い、悲しみや失望感に包まれる。

　受容：失恋を受け入れる。失恋の痛みから生まれる良い面に目を向け、目標が未来に向かい、相手との素敵な思い出とともに過去を胸にしまう。

　自分が今、この5つのステージのどこに立っているかを認識することで、前に進めるようになります。今の感情は永遠には続かないのです。

71 *Look To The Future With Hope*

Understand that when a relationship is over you will **survive and go on with your life**. Even if you cannot believe that just now, you will heal. Even if you do not believe this at the time, know that it will become true for you at some time in the future. To feel pain after loss is normal. It proves that you are alive and that you are human.

Don't stop living your life; become stronger, become hopeful that one day you will find love and happiness again. Your experience has added something to your life and will help you to look at things with more wisdom next time. In time, something good always comes from something hurtful.

---

survive and go on with your life　あなたの人生は終わりでなく、その先も続く

71. 希望を持って将来を見つめる

生きることをあきらめないことです。
その経験は次に生かされるのですから。
つらいことの後には
必ず良いことがやってくるものです。

【日本語訳】
　失恋してもあなたの人生は終わりではなく、その先も続くということを理解しましょう。今は信じられなくても、傷は癒えます。今は信じなくても、いつかはそれが現実になると知ってください。失ったときに痛みを感じるのは普通のことです。あなたが生きている証拠であり、人間である証拠なのです。
　人生を諦めないで、気持ちを強く持って、いつかあなたは愛する人を見つけ、再び幸せになれるという希望を持ちましょう。あなたの経験は人生の糧となり、次はもっと賢明に物事を見ることができるようになっているはずです。つらいことの後には必ずすぐに良いことがやってくるものです。

72 *Try Something New*

When you are ready to move forward, try doing something new or different in your life. Focus your mind on learning something new; perhaps **a musical instrument**, a new skill, new sport or interest. Try something you always wanted to do but never got around to doing.

'When I broke up with my boyfriend I started to play tennis. I always wanted to try this and never thought I had the time to spend on it. I really enjoyed it and found that I met many people at the practice sessions. It really opened up my life for me again.'

Sook

Breaking up with someone, whether after a month or a lifetime, can bring new chances and hope for you.

---

a musical instrument 楽器

72. 新しいことにチャレンジする

前に進む準備ができたなら、
何か新しいことを始めてみましょう。
きっと新しいチャンスや希望を生む
きっかけになることでしょう。

【日本語訳】
　前に進む準備ができたら、何か新しいことや違うことを始めてみましょう。新しいことを学ぶことに意識を集中して。楽器や新しいスキル、新しいスポーツや趣味など、何でも良いでしょう。以前からやってみたかったけど機会がなかったものに挑戦してみましょう。

　「彼と別れたとき、私はテニスを始めました。以前からやってみたかったんですが、そんな時間はないと思っていました。やってみると本当に楽しくて、レッスンでたくさんの人と出会えることに気づきました。テニスを始めて本当に再び未来が開けてきました」
　　　　　　　　　　　　　　　　　　　　　　　　　　　　スーク

　恋人との別れは、交際期間が短くても長くても、新しいチャンスや希望を生むきっかけになることでしょう。

73 *Do Something Kind For Someone Else*

Taking the focus from yourself and thinking about others and how you can be kind to them allows your body to heal and to get better.

Think about someone you know well or not so well and do something nice for them today. You can do it so that they know about it and can thank you or you can do it without them knowing **where the good deed came from**.

Here are some suggestions about how you can be kind to others:

- Treat everyone you know as if they are part of your family.

- Take some special treats to work/school and share them with others.

- Let the person in the line who is in a hurry be served before you.

- Open the door for someone else and smile as you do it.

- Clean out all your old clothes and give them away to people who need them.

- Help someone who is younger than you to do something that is difficult.

---

where the good deed came from その親切な行いがどこからきたのか

73. 人にやさしく

人にやさしくしてみましょう。
人へのやさしさは、
実は自分を癒やすことにつながっています。

【日本語訳】
　意識を自分から周りの人へ向けて、人に親切にする方法を考えると、体が癒され回復につながります。
　よく知っている人でも、あまり知らない人でも良いので、誰かを思い浮かべて、その人に今日何か良いことをしましょう。相手に気づかれて感謝されるようなことでも良いですし、その親切な行いがどこからきたのか相手に知られずにこっそりするのも良いでしょう。
　人に親切にするための案をいくつかご紹介します。

- 知り合い全員を家族の一員のように扱う
- 職場や学校に特別なお菓子を持って行って皆と分ける
- 列に並んでいるとき、急いでいる人に順番を譲る
- 人のために笑顔でドアを開けてあげる
- 古い洋服を処分して、必要としている人に譲る
- 自分よりも年下の人が困っていたら助けてあげる

- Tell your best friend **you appreciate her or him**.

- Next time someone speaks to you, listen carefully to their every word.

- Offer your services to do something for someone for free.

Being kind to others is also **a gentle reminder** for you to be kind to yourself. Do some of the kind things from the list above for yourself; you are worthy of feeling good about yourself.

- 親友に感謝していることを伝える
- 次に誰かが話しかけてきたら、相手の一言一言に注意深く耳を傾ける
- 誰かに無償で助けを申し出る

　人にやさしくすることは自分にもやさしくすることをそっと思い出させてくれます。上記の親切な行いを、自分にもいくつかやってみてください。あなた自身も親切な行いを受ける価値がある人なのです。

you appreciate her or him　彼女や彼に感謝している　　a gentle reminder　穏やかな合図

SECTION

7

LOVING YOURSELF

自分を好きになる

'Love is, above all else, the gift of oneself.'
Jean Anouilh

「愛とは、何よりもまず、自分という贈り物なのです」

ジャン・アヌイ

74 *How You See Yourself*

Are you kind to yourself when you think about your body, or are you unkind to yourself about your body and **how you look**?

Do you like the way you look or do you think you should be taller or prettier or thinner or have a different—looking body? If you don't like yourself now because of the way you look, you may not like yourself any better if you were able to change.

Learn to like all the good things about yourself, now. Think about all the things about yourself that you like and learn to like yourself as you are right now.

Change what you can change, but accept who and what you are right now. If you do want to change something about yourself, start with something you can change like your weight, hair style or color, general look, or **eating habits**. Set small goals for the things you can change, as well as liking yourself as you are right now.

how you look 外見　　eating habits 食生活

74. 鏡に映る自分

**もし外見が理由で自分を好きになれないのなら、
自分を好きになれる日はこれから先も
おとずれないでしょう。
まず今の自分を受け入れるのです。そして、
実現可能な小さな目標を立て実行していくのです。**

【日本語訳】
　　自分の体型について考えるとき、あなたは自分にやさしくできていますか？　それとも自分の体型や外見について、自分につらく当たってしまいますか？

　　自分の外見は好きですか？　それとも、もっと背が高くて可愛くて細くて違う体型が良かったと思っていますか？　外見のせいで今の自分を好きになれないと、たとえ変われたとしても自分のことを好きにはなれないかもしれません。

　　今の自分の長所を好きになれるようにしましょう。あなた自身の好きなところはどこかを考えてみて、今のあなたを好きになれるようにしましょう。

　　変えられるところは変え、今の自分を受け入れるのです。何かを変えたいのなら、まずは変えられるものから始めましょう。例えば、体重やヘアスタイル、ヘアカラー、全般的な外見、食生活など。変えられるものについて小さな目標を設定すると同時に、今現在のあなた自身を好きになりましょう。

75 *Don't Compare Yourself With Others*

The media often write about the wealth and beauty of rock stars and movie stars, sports people and authors. These people have become people we **look up to**. Papers and websites are often full of stories and pictures about these 'perfect' people with 'perfect' bodies and lives. Do you really believe all these stories?

It is too easy for women to feel like failures when they **measure themselves against famous people**.

You may also think that the people you know, your friends and people you work with, are more beautiful or smarter than you.

You are a special person; no one is like you. Whatever you are right now is special. You must learn to accept and like yourself rather than being unkind to yourself by measuring yourself against other people.

---

don't compare yourself with others 自分を他人と比べない   look up to あこ
がれる   measure themselves against famous people 有名人と自分を比べる

75. 他人と比べない

自分を他人と比べるのは、やめましょう。
芸能人や友人と比べてよいことなど
何もありません。
あなたは特別な存在なのです。
どこにもあなたのような人はいないのです。

【日本語訳】
　メディアは、ロックスターや映画スター、スポーツ選手、作家の富や美しさを取り上げます。彼らは私たちのあこがれの存在になっています。新聞やウェブサイトにはよく、これらの「完璧な」人々の「完璧な」ボディーや暮らしの記事が、写真付きで掲載されています。あなたは本当にこれらの記事を信じていますか？
　女性は有名人と自分を比べて、自分が失敗作かのように感じてしまいがちです。
　知人や友人、同僚のほうが、自分よりも美しく賢いと思っているかもしれません。
　あなたは特別な人です。誰一人あなたのような人はいません。あなたが今どんな人でも、あなたは特別なのです。人と比べて自分につらく当たるのではなく、自分自身を受け入れて好きになることを学びましょう。

76 *Be Positive About Yourself*

It is healthy to think and feel positive about yourself. Here are some things you can do to feel positive about yourself:

- Accept that you are not perfect and you never will be.
- Look at the positive, the many things that are good about you.
- Be grateful for the good things already in your life.
- Don't think about the future too much.
- Have a dream for the future, but live now.
- Relax, **let go of worry**.
- Care for yourself and others.
- Meet people and make friends.

Learn to laugh more and play; have fun with your partner and friends.

---

let go of worry 不安を取り除く

76. 自分にポジティブになる

**自分に対してポジティブに感じることは
よいことです。
彼や友人とともに、
笑い、遊び、大いに楽しむのです。**

【日本語訳】
　自分自身に対してポジティブな考えや気持ちを持つことは健康的なことです。自分自身にポジティブな気持ちを持つためにできることを、以下にご紹介します。

- あなたは完璧ではなく、完璧にはなれないということを受け入れる
- あなた自身のポジティブな、たくさんの良い面に目を向ける
- あなたがこれまでの人生で手に入れたものに感謝する
- 未来のことを考えすぎない
- 将来の夢を持ちつつ、今を生きる
- リラックスして不安を取り除く
- 自分と他人にやさしくする
- 人に会って仲良くなる

もっと笑って遊びましょう。彼や友人と楽しいことをしましょう。

77 *Mistakes Are Great*

Everyone makes choices about their lives that sometimes don't **work out** for them. Everyone makes mistakes every day. When you make a mistake, the most important thing is not to be too unkind to yourself. Learn from these mistakes, and use every thing that happens to you as **a learning point**.

Welcome mistakes in your life. When you know about a mistake and accept that you have made it you can learn from it. Forgive yourself about making mistakes and learn what to do and what not to do next time.

That's the gift a mistake can give you—the gift of learning about yourself and about what you could do better and more wisely next time.

---

work out うまくいく   **a learning point** 学びの場

77. 失敗はすばらしいこと

誰でも毎日のように間違いを犯します。
ですがそのことで自分を責めすぎてはいけません。
私たちはそこから次への教訓を学べるのです。

【日本語訳】
　　誰しもが誤って、自分にとってうまくいかない人生の選択を
してしまうことがあります。人は毎日失敗をします。失敗をし
たら、一番大切なことは自分につらく当たらないことです。失
敗から学び、あなたに起こるすべてのことを学びの場として活
かしましょう。
　　あなたの人生に失敗を歓迎しましょう。失敗に気づいて、自
分が失敗したことを受け入れたら、そこから学ぶことができま
す。失敗をした自分を許し、次は何をするべきで、何をするべ
きでないかを学びましょう。
　　教訓は失敗が与えてくれるプレゼントです。自分自身につい
て学び、次はどうすれば良くなるか、どうすればもっと賢い選
択ができるかを学ぶことができるのです。

78 *Don't Beat Yourself Up About Mistakes*

What do you say to yourself when you make a mistake? Is it mostly good and positive, as it would be if you were talking to a friend? Or is what you say to yourself negative and hurtful?

Learning to love yourself when you make mistakes is one of the most important things you will ever do. Everyone makes mistakes; this is how you really learn about yourself and the world. Mistakes can make you more **understanding** and teach you to be a better person. Most people learn and grow through making mistakes and then they change what they do next time.

Be open to learn from mistakes so you may learn and grow as a person.

---

understanding　寛大な　　be open to learn from mistakes　心を広く持ち失敗から学ぶ

78. 失敗した自分を責めない

失敗したときにも、
自分自身にやさしくしてあげましょう。
失敗しない人などいません。
私たちは失敗から学び、成長していくのです。

【日本語訳】
　失敗をしたとき、あなたは自分にどんな言葉をかけますか？　友人にかけるようなポジティブで良い言葉ですか？　それとも、ネガティブで厳しい言葉ですか？

　失敗をしたときに自分のことを好きになれるようにすることは、あなたがするべき一番大切なことです。誰でも失敗はします。失敗をして自分自身と世の中について本当の意味で学ぶのです。失敗はあなたの心を寛大にし、より良い人間になれるよう教えてくれます。人は失敗から学んで成長し、次に取る行動を変えるのです。

　心を広く持ち失敗から学ぶことで、人として成長できるのです。

79 *Be Careful About Who You Spend Time With*

Do people around you speak badly about themselves or about others when you are with them? Do they say unpleasant things about what they or others look like or how or what they eat?

Being around people like this can make you feel bad. If your friends don't think the same way you think or the way you want to think, you can change who you spend time with.

It may not be easy to spend less time with people you are used to being with, but if they don't support the way you think and feel about yourself and your body, then **for your own health and well being** it may be better for you not to be with them

---

for your own health and well being　あなたの心と体の健康のため

79. 一緒に過ごす人に注意する

いつも一緒にいる人が
あなたを嫌な気持ちにさせるなら、
相手を変えることです。
それはあなたの心と体の健康のためになります。

【日本語訳】
　周りの人たちはあなたといるときに自分のことや他人のこと
を悪く言ったりしますか？　自分や他人の外見や食事のしかた、
食べるものについて不愉快なことを言ったりしますか？
　そのような人たちと一緒にいると、あなたまで嫌な気持ちに
なりかねません。友人があなたとは考え方が違ったり、あなた
が良いと思う考え方を持っていないなら、一緒に過ごす相手を
変えましょう。
　今まで一緒にいた人たちと過ごす時間を減らすことは簡単で
はないかもしれません。ですが、あなた自身やあなたの体につ
いてのあなたの考えや気持ちを支持してくれない人たちなら、
一緒にいないほうがあなたの心と体の健康のためなのです。

80 *Have A Healthy Body*

It is not unusual to hear a teenager and her mother speak the same way about food and exercise because they have the same beliefs about food and exercise.

The same can be said about you and your friends. The way you and others speak and feel about your body has an impact on your attitude toward how you feel and look. Find the company of friends who have a healthy attitude toward their bodies and how they look after and care for them.

It is easy to reflect the values and beliefs of those you spend time with. Be with people who **have a healthy relationship** with food and their body. For just as you take good things from what you eat, you also take the views, whether good or bad, of those you spend time with.

have a healthy relationship　健康的な関わり方

80. 健康な体

食べるものに意識を向け、
自分の体を大切にしている友人を持ちましょう。
彼らと過ごすことで、
あなたの感じ方やものの見方に、
よい影響がもたらされるでしょう。

【日本語訳】
　食べ物や運動について10代の子とその母親の意見が同じということはよくあります。それは、食べ物や運動についての考え方が同じだからです。
　あなたと友人についても同じことが言えます。体型についてあなたと友人が話すことや感じることは、外見に対するあなたの感じ方や姿勢に影響を与えます。体型や体のケアに健康的に向き合っている友人とつき合いましょう。
　人は一緒にいる人たちの価値観や意見に染まりやすいものです。食べ物や体のケアについて健康的な関わり方をしている人たちとつき合いましょう。食べ物から栄養を吸収するように、考え方も（良いものも悪いものも）あなたが一緒に過ごす人から吸収するのです。

81 Don't Be Competitive With Friends

Some people want to be better than their friends in all areas of their lives. They are competitive in sports, work, how many friends they have, how much money they spend or the way they look. **They compete with their friends** to be better than them rather than enjoy them.

Men mainly try to be better than each other in sport and work. Women try to be better than other women more quietly with body shape, body size and beauty.

Try to spend time with people who are not trying to be better than you. Find people who have good, balanced values and who like you the way you are.

---

they compete with their friends 彼らは友人と張り合う

81. 友人と競わない

**自分が友人より優れていないとおさまらない
という人がいます。
そういう人とはつき合わないことです。
あなたのあるがままを受け入れてくれる
友人を見つけましょう。**

【日本語訳】
　人生のあらゆる面で友人に勝とうとする人がいます。スポーツでも仕事でも、友人の数でも、使うお金の金額でも、外見でも他人と競います。彼らは友人関係を楽しむよりも、勝つために友人と張り合います。

　男性は主にスポーツや仕事で相手に勝とうとします。女性は体型や体のサイズ、美しさで静かに競います。

　あなたと張り合おうとしない人たちと一緒に過ごすよう心がけましょう。バランスの取れた良い価値観を持っていて、ありのままのあなたを好きになってくれる友人を見つけましょう。

82
Move Your Body

Exercise is a positive way to help your body to feel good. Find what exercises you like and that help make you feel good about yourself.

Exercise can be simple. Walk some of the distance to work, take the time to get off your bus or train one stop earlier on your journey and walk the rest of the way. This is a small but positive way to exercise your body.

Walk up the stairs instead of using the elevator. Ride a bike or walk to work or to the shops instead of going by car, bus or train. Try **yoga** for 30 minutes a day; this is simple exercise that is very good for you. **Practice breathing well**.

Exercise allows your body to feel well and happy.

---

yoga ヨガ　　Practice breathing well. 良い呼吸法を練習しましょう。

82. 体を動かす

心と体を健康に保つために
エクササイズをしましょう。
ひと駅前で降りて歩く、
エレベーターでなく階段を使うなど、
簡単なものでよいのです。

【日本語訳】
　運動は体を健康に保つ良い方法です。あなたの好きな、気分が良くなる運動を見つけましょう。

　運動は簡単なもので大丈夫です。通勤の一部を徒歩に変える、バスや電車をひと駅前で降りて歩く、など。これらはちょっとしたことですが、体を動かす良い方法です。

　エレベーターを使う代わりに階段を上りましょう。車やバス、電車に乗らずに自転車や徒歩で仕事や買い物に行きましょう。一日に30分ヨガを試してみるのもいいでしょう。簡単な運動ですが、これが健康にとても良いのです。良い呼吸法を練習しましょう。

　運動はあなたの体を健康で幸せにしてくれます。

83 *Relax*

Relaxing is a big part of caring for your body. There are other ways to relax than reading and watching television. Relaxation can be about taking some time out from actively doing things all the time.

You can relax and lessen stress by doing the following:

- Lie down and relax your body.
- Close your eyes.
- **Let go of any stress**.
- **Uncross your arms and legs**.
- Take some deep breaths, hold each breath for a couple of seconds and let it go.
- Allow your body to relax.
- Think about each part of your body in turn and let go of any stress you may feel in that part of your body.
- Try not to think thoughts that worry or stress you.
- **Let your body feel calm**.
- Enjoy this feeling.

Try to stay that way for at least five minutes. Do this once or twice every day.

Let go of any stress. ストレスを解放させましょう　Uncross your arms and legs. 腕や脚を組むのをやめましょう。　Let your body feel calm. 体を落ち着かせましょう。

83. リラックス

リラックスして体をいたわりましょう。
1日に一度か二度、
そのための時間を持つことです。

【日本語訳】
　リラックスは体のケアにおいて重要です。本を読んだりテレビを観たりする以外にも、リラックスする方法はあります。短時間だけでも、常に忙しく何かをするのをやめることもリラックスです。

　リラックスとストレス解消の方法を以下にご紹介します。

- 横になって体をリラックスさせる
- 目を閉じる
- ストレスを解放させる
- 腕や脚を組むのをやめる
- 深呼吸をして数秒間息を止め、吐き出す
- 全身の力を抜く
- 体の各部に順番に意識を向け、その部位に感じるストレスを解放させる
- 心配事やストレスの種について考えないようにする
- 体を落ち着かせる
- この感覚を楽しむ

　その状態を少なくとも5分間保ちましょう。これを1日に一度か二度行いましょう。

84 *Have Fun*

When you relax your body you feel good about yourself. Having fun is another way to relax and enjoy yourself. This can mean doing good things like:

- Cook the food you like.

- Take a holiday.

- Clean your home and **make it special**.

- Have nice things around you.

- Get some flowers for your home.

- Go to the movies.

- Play the music you love.

- Be kind to yourself every day.

- Read, draw, write, play, laugh and walk more.

'I love to draw pictures of trees and flowers. I'm not much good at it, but it's so **unlike what I do** in my job all day, every day. This is my way to let go and have fun.'

Tina

What do you enjoy doing? What helps you to **feel lighter** and happier? How could you do more of this in your life?

---

make it special 特別なものにする　　**unlike what I do** やっていることとかけ離れている　　**feel lighter** 心が軽くなる

84. 楽しみを持つ

積極的に楽しいことをして、
リラックスしましょう。
心が軽くなり、楽しめることは何でしょうか？

【日本語訳】
　体をリラックスさせると気分が良くなります。楽しみを持つこともリラックスして楽しく過ごすもう1つの方法です。良い例をいくつかご紹介します。

- 食べたいものを作る
- 休みを取る
- 家を掃除して特別な空間にする
- 身の回りに素敵な物を置く
- 家に花を飾る
- 映画に行く
- 好きな音楽をかける
- 毎日自分にやさしくする
- もっと本を読み、絵を描き、文章を書き、遊び、笑い、歩く

「私は木や花の絵を描くのが好きです。上手ではないけれど、毎日長時間やっている仕事とはかけ離れているところがいいんです。これが私のストレス解消法であり、楽しく過ごす方法です」

ティナ

　あなたは何をするのが好きですか？　心が軽くなり、幸せを感じるものは？　それをもっとたくさんやるには、どうすれば良いでしょうか？

85 *Sit Well And Stand Tall*

Almost everyone uses a computer these days; emails and the Internet have made computers a big part of our lives. Also, your computer is often used as part of your study or work or leisure time. This can have a poor effect on the way you sit and the way you stand. **Leaning over a computer** can cause **stress and discomfort**. When you are at the computer, remember to sit up straight and relax your shoulders and place your feet flat on the floor; don't cross your legs.

It's the same with standing. Many people stand in their work or have to stand for a long time during the day. Stand up straight and tall as it is important for **good health and wellness**.

Both sitting well and standing straight are good for your breathing too.

---

leaning over a computer パソコンに向かって前かがみの姿勢をとる　　stress and
discomfort ストレスや不快感　　good health and wellness 健やかな心と体

85. きちんと座り、姿勢良く立つ

パソコンの前に座りっぱなしになっていませんか。
背筋を伸ばしてまっすぐ立っていますか。
正しく座り、立つことは、
あなたの呼吸も楽にします。

【日本語訳】
　現代ではほとんど誰もがパソコンを使っています。メールや
インターネットの普及により、パソコンは私たちの暮らしの大
きな一部となりました。また、パソコンは学校や職場、自由時
間にもよく使われています。パソコンの使用は、座ったり立っ
たりする姿勢に悪影響を与えることがあります。パソコンに向
かって前かがみの姿勢をとると、ストレスや不快感の原因とな
ります。パソコンの前に座っているときは、姿勢良く座って肩
の力を抜き、床に足を平らについて脚を組まないよう心がけま
しょう。
　立っているときも同じです。多くの人が立ち仕事をしたり、
一日のうちの長い時間を立って過ごします。姿勢良く立つこと
は健やかな心と体のために重要です。
　きちんと座り、姿勢良く立つと、呼吸も楽になります。

86 *Learn To Breathe Correctly*

Breathing is easy; you don't have to think about it, it just happens. How do you breathe most of the time? Long deep breaths or short sharp breaths, or **somewhere in between**?

Most of us breathe short breaths most of the time, but breathing like this all the time does not look after your body as well as breathing deeply does. When you breathe deeply it centers your body and helps you to relax.

If you want to check how you are breathing do the following;

- Lie down. Put a book on your **stomach** and another book on your **chest.**

- Take a deep breath.

- If the book on your stomach rises higher than the one on your chest you are breathing as deeply as you could.

Every day, be more aware of how you breathe, especially when you are stressed or worried. Breathing deeply almost always **calms your body and your mind**.

---

somewhere in between　その中間くらい　　stomach　お腹　　chest　胸
calms your body and your mind　体と心を落ち着かせる

86. 正しく呼吸する

呼吸に意識を向けるようにしましょう。
深い呼吸はあなたの体や心を落ち着かせます。

【日本語訳】

　　呼吸は簡単です。考えなくても無意識にできます。あなたは普段どのように呼吸をしていますか？　長く深い呼吸ですか？それとも短く鋭い呼吸ですか？　その中間くらいですか？

　　多くの人が普段、短い呼吸をしています。しかし、このような呼吸は深い呼吸と比べて体に良くありません。深い呼吸は体に意識を向け、リラックスを促します。

　　自分がどのような呼吸をしているか確認するには、以下の方法を試してみてください。

- 横になります。お腹の上と胸の上に本を1冊ずつ置きます。
- 深呼吸をします。
- お腹の上の本が胸の上の本よりも高い位置に来たら、可能な限り深く呼吸できている証拠です。

　　毎日、呼吸にもっと意識を向けましょう。特に、ストレスや不安を感じているときはこれが重要です。深い呼吸は、ほぼ必ず体と心を落ち着かせてくれます。

87 *Time For Yourself*

Do you make time for yourself? Do you have times where you do things just for you?

Our work culture **has placed a high value on paid work**. Everyone works longer hours at their everyday jobs so it may not feel natural to spend time for yourself by yourself. Some people make their relaxation time **as busy as a work day**. They fit in so much that they never seem to stop doing things, either at work or in their own time.

Allow quiet time for yourself; it is very healthy to treat yourself in this way.

---

has placed a high value on paid work　お金になる仕事を価値あるものとしてきた　　as busy as a work day　仕事の日と同じくらい忙しく

87. 自分のための時間

自分だけの時間を持っていますか。
自分だけの静かなひとときを確保することは、
とても大切なことなのです。

【日本語訳】

　　あなたは自分のために時間を作っていますか？　自分のため
だけに何かをする時間はありますか？

　　現代の労働文化は、お金になる仕事を価値のあるものとして
きました。誰もが毎日職場で長時間働いているため、自分のた
めにひとりの時間を過ごすことを、当然のこととは感じられな
いかもしれません。リラックスタイムに仕事の日と同じくらい
忙しく過ごす人もいます。彼らは仕事の日も休みの日も変わら
ず、用事を詰め込み忙しく動き回ります。

　　自分のために静かな時間を持ちましょう。自分にこのような
ご褒美をあげることは、とても健康的なことです。

88 *Do You Get Too Stressed?*

Do you sometimes **feel stressed out**? Do you worry about things in your life that you can do nothing about? Do you feel negative sometimes? Or worry about work, family and friends? Are you afraid to meet new people sometimes? Do you sometimes feel worried about the future?

If any of these things happen to you there is something you can do to help yourself. Try to think about the good things that happen around you, not just the negative things. Do one small thing at a time and be happy to do that.

Relax your thinking as well as your body.

Talk to someone you trust about your feelings and fears or **write a journal or a diary** about how you feel. Think most about the present, not the past or the future. You may like to exercise more, or walk every day. These are all good ways to start feeling good about yourself.

feel stressed out ストレスが溜まる　　write a journal or a diary 手帳や日記を書く

88. ストレス過剰

ストレスに押しつぶされていませんか。
過去や未来のことを考えるのではなく、
今に思いを巡らしましょう。

【日本語訳】
　ストレスが溜まることはありますか？　あなたにはどうしようもないことを心配することはありますか？　ネガティブな気持ちになることは？　仕事や家族、友人について悩むことは？初めての人と会うことが不安になることは？　将来について不安になることは？

　このような状況に陥ったときに、自分のためにできることがあります。ネガティブなことだけではなく、周りで起きている良いことについて考えるようにしましょう。一度に1つだけ小さなことをして、そのことに満足しましょう。

　思考と体をリラックスさせましょう。

　信頼する人にあなたの気持ちや心配事について話したり、感じたことを手帳や日記に書いたりしましょう。過去や未来のことではなく、現在のことを主に考えましょう。もっと運動をしたり、毎日歩いたりしましょう。これらは気分を良くする素晴らしい方法です。

89 *Nurture A Healthy Self-image*

Your self-image is how you see yourself. This is different from how you feel about yourself, which is self-esteem. Is your self-view real about the whole of you—your skills at work, how you look, your relationship skills, your energy, your goals, your friendliness and your **compassion**?

To help you **develop a realistic self-image**, write two lists. Write one with your strengths (things you are good at) and one with your weaknesses (things you would like to change or do better).

When you start, the weaknesses list is likely to be longer than the strengths. When you really think about yourself you will be surprised to find that there are so many strengths, so many good things about you. Don't overlook things you might think are small; it is strength to be able to do your work well, keep your home in good order, to be a good friend to someone, to be kind to a pet, to tell the truth.

Think about these strengths every day as this builds a healthy and realistic self-image that will help you to feel good about yourself.

nurture a healty self-image 健全なセルフイメージを育む   compassion 思いや
り   develop a realistic self-image 現実的なセルフイメージを構築する

89. 健全なセルフイメージを育む

よいセルフイメージを持ちましょう。
自分の長所は何かを考えるよう心がけましょう。
リストアップしていくと、
たくさんの長所に気づくはずです。

【日本語訳】
　あなたのセルフイメージは、あなたが自分をどう見ているかを表します。これはあなた自身のことをどう感じるか、つまり自尊心とは異なります。あなたのセルフイメージは本当のあなたですか？　あなたの職場でのスキルやあなたの外見、コミュニケーションスキル、エネルギー、目標、人当たりの良さ、思いやりなどを表していますか？

　現実的なセルフイメージを構築するために、2つのリストを作成しましょう。1つにはあなたの長所（得意なこと）、もう1つには短所（変えたいことや改善したいこと）を書きます。

　最初は短所のリストのほうが長所のリストより長くなるでしょう。でも、自分のことをもっと真剣に考えるうちに、あなたはたくさんの長所を持っていて、良いところがたくさんあることに驚くでしょう。些細なことに思えることも見逃さないで。仕事ができるところ、家の中をきれいに保てるところ、良い友であれるところ、ペットにやさしいところ、嘘をつかないところなど、どれもが長所です。

　これらの長所について毎日考えましょう。そうすることで、健康的で現実的なセルフイメージを構築することができ、自分に自信が持てるようになるのです。

90 *Build Your Self-esteem*

It's important to feel good and to be clear and strong about your skills and about what you can do.

No one is perfect, but **you are mostly capable**. Remember that you have good skills in your work, you have some relationship skills and you can talk clearly, listen and **achieve your goals**. You may not fit the popular magazine pictures for size, figure, dress and the bag you carry, but you can still dress well, or buy nice things. While there may be a few things you would like to change about yourself, you are probably more OK **than you think you are**.

When you think about yourself, do you like yourself? Do you see yourself as positively as you really are? Do you feel mostly good about yourself? Do you have good self-esteem? Or do you talk badly to yourself about **those few things you might like to improve about yourself**?

To help with this, think about your strengths, the things you are good at. Think about the things you do well each day rather than talking badly to yourself about any small things you could have done better.

---

you are mostly capable あなたはだいたいできている　　achieve your goals
目標を達成する　　than you think you are あなたが思う自分より　　those few
things you might like to improve about yourself 自分自身の改善したいちょっと
した部分

90. 自尊心を持つ

自分に自信を持つことはとても大切です。
完璧な人などいないのですから。
できないことに目を向けるのではなく、
自分ができていることを見つめるのです。

【日本語訳】
　あなたの持っているスキルや得意なことを明確にし、自信を持つことが大切です。

　完璧な人などいませんが、あなたはだいたいできているのです。あなたは仕事で優れたスキルを持っていて、コミュニケーションスキルもあり、分かりやすく話し、相手の言葉に耳を傾け、目標を達成することができます。人気雑誌の写真のような体型や顔、ドレスやバッグは持っていなくても、おしゃれをしたり素敵な物を買ったりすることはできます。自分について変えたい部分はいくつかあるかもしれませんが、あなたはあなたが思う自分よりも良いはずです。

　あなたは自分のことを考えるとき、自分のことが好きですか？あなたは実際のあなたと同じくらいポジティブに自分のことを見ていますか？　あなたは自分のことをだいたい気に入っていますか？　あなたは良い自尊心を持っていますか？　それとも、自分自身の改善したいちょっとした部分について自分にケチをつけていますか？

　これを改善するためには、あなたの長所、得意なことについて考えましょう。毎日、もっとうまくできたかもしれない些細なことについて自分にケチをつける代わりに、うまくできたことについて考えましょう。

91 *Take Control*

The things you hear from others, the words you speak to others and the words you speak to yourself can all **make a difference to you,** to your life and your thoughts.

If you hear negative things all the time, you are more likely to become negative in your thinking and your actions. If you often say hard or unkind things about others, you are likely to become hard and unkind in your own heart.

You can control your own thoughts and stop negative thinking. You also can choose to control how people talk to you. If people around you often say negative or unpleasant things, you can either ask them to change what they are talking about or not listen to them. You will be a stronger and better person if you do this.

make a difference to you あなたに影響を及ぼす

91. コントロールする

**ネガティブな言葉とは距離を保ちましょう。
それはあなたの考え方や行動に
影響を及ぼします。**

【日本語訳】
　他人から聞かされる言葉や、あなた自身が他人や自分に話す言葉は、あなた自身やあなたの人生、あなたの思考に影響を及ぼします。

　常にネガティブな言葉を聞いていると、あなたの思考も行動もネガティブなものになります。他人について厳しく思いやりのないことを言っていると、あなたの心も厳しく思いやりのないものになります。

　あなたは、あなた自身の思考をコントロールし、ネガティブな思考を止めることができます。また、あなたは、あなたに対する他人の話し方をコントロールすることもできます。周りの人がよくネガティブで不快なことを言う人ならば、彼らに話題を変えるよう頼むか、耳を傾けるのをやめましょう。そうすることであなたは、もっと強く良い人間になることができるのです。

92 *Don't Shoot The Messenger!*

When someone tells you something, there are two separate parts to the message you hear. The first part is what is said and the second part is what you think and feel at the time about the person who brings you the message.

There is a saying, 'Don't shoot the messenger.' This saying comes from stories told in the history of war. **When bad news was delivered**, the general would have the messenger shot so that the soldiers would not find out about this bad news.

If you do not like what is in the message, try not to be angry about it, try not to put **all your attention** on the person giving it. It is very important not to focus only on the person who brings the message. As the saying goes, 'Don't shoot the messenger.' They are not the problem.

Think about what you can learn from each message. Is there some part of what is said that you should think about? Sometimes the message isn't about you at all, or it may be wrong. It may show the feelings of the person who brings the message, rather than be something about you.

Try to think about what information could be useful for you, and leave the rest alone. But **in any case**, don't shoot the messenger!

Don't shoot the messenger! メッセンジャーを撃つな！　when bad news was delivered 悪い知らせが届けられると　all your attention 全意識　in any case いずれにせよ

92. メッセンジャーを撃たない

**あなたが望まないことを言った人を恨んでは
いけません。言われた内容と、言った人とを
切り離して考えることが必要です。**

【日本語訳】

　誰かがあなたに何かを伝えるとき、あなたの耳に届くメッセージには2つの部分があります。1つ目は言われた言葉、2つ目はメッセージを届けてくれた人に対してそのときあなたが考えたり感じたりすることです。

　英語のことわざに「Don't shoot the messenger（メッセンジャーを撃つな）」というものがあります。このことわざは戦時中の言い伝えから来たものです。悪い知らせが届けられると、司令官は兵士たちにその悪い知らせを知られないようにメッセンジャーを撃ち殺させたといいます。

　伝言の内容が気に入らなかったとしても、そのことに腹を立てず、それを伝えてくれた相手に怒りの矛先を向けないようにしましょう。伝言を告げた相手に全意識を集中させないことがとても大切です。ことわざのとおり、「メッセンジャーを撃つな」です。問題はメッセンジャーではないのです。

　それぞれのメッセージから学べることを考えてみましょう。伝えられたメッセージの中に、あなたが考えるべき部分はありますか？　そもそもそのメッセージは、全くあなたのことを言っているのではなかったり、間違っている場合もあります。あなた自身のことではなく、それを伝える人の気持ちを表しているのかもしれません。

　どんな情報があなたの役に立ちそうかを考え、それ以外は無視するようにしましょう。いずれにせよ、「メッセンジャーを撃つな」です。

93 *Learn To Like Yourself*

Many women think that the love of a man will make them happy. Some women fear being alone because they see it as **shameful**. The truth of it is that women are very strong and can be happy living on their own. When you learn to live with yourself and like yourself you truly become strong.

It is possible to be just as alone when you are with someone in a relationship as when you are not with someone; when you are with someone who is making you unhappy you can feel very alone.

Learn to like yourself because this **builds good feelings** about yourself and helps you to feel good no matter who is or isn't in your life.

---

shameful 恥ずかしい　　builds good feelings 自信を持つ

93. 自分を好きになること

ひとりで幸せでいられる女性は、
本当に強い女性です。
それはパートナーがいる、いないに
関係ないことなのです。

【日本語訳】
　多くの女性が、男性に愛されることで幸せになれると考えています。ひとりでいることは恥ずかしいことだと考えて、ひとりになるのを恐れる女性もいます。でも、実際には、女性はとても強いのでひとりでも幸せに生きることができます。良心に恥じないように生き、自分を好きになる方法を学んだら、本当の意味で強くなれます。
　交際している人がいても、ひとりでいるのと同じように孤独なこともあります。あなたを不幸に感じさせる相手と一緒にいると、ひどく孤独を感じることがあるからです。
　自分を好きになることを学びましょう。そうすることで、自分に自信が持てるようになり、パートナーがいる、いないに関わらず気分良く過ごせるようになります。

94 *When You Are On Your Own You Can Learn And Grow*

It's OK if you are alone at the moment, if you are not in a relationship. Whether it is for a short time or a lifetime, it can **provide a great space for you to learn and grow**.

Being **on your own** for some time may well be just the right thing for you to give you the chance to think about what you really want and who you really are. If you have been hurt before, being on your own can heal you and help you to feel strong again.

Trust yourself if you are on your own and you will learn and grow as a person.

provide a great space for you to learn and grow　学びと成長の機会を与える
on your own　自分ひとりで

94. ひとりで学び成長する

自分を見つめるためにひとりでいることは
正しいことです。
それはあなたに、
人間としての成長をもたらす力となります。

【日本語訳】
　今、あなたがひとりでも、交際している人がいなくても大丈夫です。ひとりでいることは、期間の長短を問わず、あなたに学びと成長の機会を与えてくれます。

　しばらくひとりになることは、あなたにとって正しいことかもしれません。自分が本当は何を求めていて、どんな人なのかを知るために、考える機会を与えてくれるからです。失恋の傷を負った人は、ひとりになることで傷を癒やし、強さを取り戻すことができるでしょう。

　ひとりでいても自分自身を信じれば、人として学び、成長することができるのです。

95 *Connect With Yourself*

Take time to **nurture yourself. Get in touch with your inner self**, your inner wisdom.

Being still is a great way to get in touch with the real you. When you stop thinking and just sit and **let your mind drift**, you create a space for your inner self to breathe, creating a rich inner life, a life that isn't about other people and action, just about you and your inner true self. Each person has their own way of connecting with this inner part of themselves. Try your own way to find some space and time to stop and **let go of everyday life**.

'When I sit still and stop thinking, there is this other part of me who is just kind of happy and **at ease with myself**, just sitting doing nothing. This is my inner self. I feel better about myself when I make time to sit quietly and let go of my mind trying to make sense of everything all the time. When I make time to do that I am a much happier person and much less stressed.'

Kylie

---

connect with yourself 自分とつながる　　nurture yourself 自分を成長させる
get in touch with your inner self 内なる自分とつながる　　let your mind drift
あなたの心を漂わせる　　let go of everyday life 日常を忘れる　　at ease with
myself ひとりでリラックスして

95. 自分とつながる

**内なる自分と触れ合う時間を持ちましょう。
考えるのをやめて、静かに座り、
心を解放するのです。**

【日本語訳】
　自分を成長させる時間を取りましょう。内なる自分、内なる心の声とつながりましょう。

　本当のあなたとつながるためには、じっとしていることが有効です。考えるのをやめて、ただ座って心を漂わせ、内なる自分に呼吸をする余裕を与えましょう。他人や行動にとらわれない、あなただけの、本来の自分が中心にいる豊かな内なる人生を創るのです。内なる自分とつながる方法は人それぞれです。あなた独自の方法で、立ち止まって日常を忘れる空間と時間を見つけましょう。

　「ただじっと座って考えるのをやめたとき、ひとりでリラックスするちょっぴり幸せなもうひとりの自分がいます。何もしないでただじっと座って過ごすのです。これが私の内なる自分です。静かに座る時間を作って、常にすべてのことに意味を見出そうとする思考から自分を解放するのです。そうすると、私はずっと幸せな気分になり、ストレスがぐっと軽減されます」

カイリー

96   *Your Needs Are Important*

Make time in your diary each week just for you. You can do anything you want with this time as long as you keep that time for yourself. Unless you live away from everything, there is usually some sort of noise going on around you, even if it is just **the quiet hum of a computer**. Trains, cars, people, television and loud music all make the world around you a busy place to be.

Time alone is a caring and very supporting thing to do for yourself. Start with two minutes a day and build this up to a longer time.

It is just as important to make this time whether you are a student, in paid work or not; making time for yourself **improves your sense of real value and self worth**. When you spend time by yourself your values will become clearer and **more certain**. Time alone will help you to be clear about your values and what you want in your life.

---

the quiet hum of a computer パソコンの小さなモーター音 improves your
sense of real value and self worth あなたの真の価値観や自尊心を養う more
certain より確固としたもの

96. 必要なことが大切なこと

自分のためだけに使う時間を確保しましょう。
騒がしい日常から離れて過ごすことで、
本当の価値観や自尊心が
養われるようになるのです。

【日本語訳】
　　毎週自分だけの時間を作って手帳に書き込みましょう。この時間には何をしても構いませんが、必ずひとりで過ごすこと。辺境にでも住んでいない限り、たいていあなたの周りには、何らかのノイズがあります。それがたとえ、パソコンの小さなモーター音だとしても。電車、車、人、テレビ、大音量の音楽などすべてが、あなたのいる世界を忙しい場所にします。
　　ひとりの時間は自分をケアし、支えるための素晴らしい方法です。1日2分から始めて、だんだん伸ばしていきましょう。
　　学生でも社会人でも関係なく、こうしたひとりの時間を取ることは大切です。ひとりの時間を作ることで、あなたの真の価値観や自尊心が養われるようになるのです。ひとりで過ごすと、あなたの価値観が明確になり、確固としたものになります。ひとりの時間を持つことで、あなたの価値観やあなたが人生に望むものを明確にすることができるのです。

97   *Balance Your Needs*

It is easy to care about other people's needs and forget about your own needs. Do you care too much about what other people suggest you do or ask you to do, and not enough about your own needs?

Some women believe their value is about doing things for other people to please them or to make them like you.

Sometimes women find it easier to let go of the time they have **set aside** for themselves because it is easier to do this than tell someone else they are going to keep this time for themselves. Sometimes it seems easier to let other people's needs be more important than your own; easier to **give in** to someone else's needs than your own.

When you make time for yourself you will help to keep your life in balance.

---

set aside　とっておく　　give in　諦める

97. ときには自分を優先する

**人のことばかりを優先して、
自分のことを後回しにしていませんか。
自分の時間を大切にすると、
人生がバランスのとれたものになっていきます。**

【日本語訳】

　人は他人のことばかり優先して自分のことを後回しにしがちです。人から受けた提案や頼みごとばかり気にして、自分のことをおざなりにしていませんか？

　人のために何かをして人を喜ばせることや、人に好かれることが自分の価値だと信じている女性もいます。

　自分のためにとっておいた時間なのに、そのことを相手に伝えるよりも楽だからという理由で、自分の時間を簡単に諦める女性もいます。自分のニーズよりも誰かのニーズを優先するほうが簡単に思えることがあります。人のニーズのために自分のニーズを諦めるほうが簡単なのです。

　自分のための時間を確保すると、人生がバランスの取れたものになっていきます。

98 *Your Best Friend*

If you were married to you, how long would you stay married? You need to be mostly positive to keep a relationship with someone else strong, but do you know how to keep a happy and positive relationship with yourself?

Everyone knows that to be healthy they need to look after themselves. You can care for yourself in **many physical ways**. But how do you care for yourself in your thoughts and feelings? Are you kind to yourself in the way that you think about yourself? Do you think kind, loving thoughts about yourself? Do you like yourself? Are you having any fun yet?

Doing things to care for yourself is a positive habit. Being kind to one's self is a way to care for your relationship with yourself. Caring and being kind needs practice to become a lifelong habit. It is completely an inside job.

---

many physical ways 身体的にさまざまな方法で

98. ベストフレンド

**自分のことを大切にする習慣を持ちましょう。
体だけでなく、自分の心にも気を配りましょう。**

【日本語訳】

　自分自身と結婚したら、結婚生活はどのくらい長続きすると思いますか？　誰かとの関係を強く保ちたいなら、普段からポジティブでいることが必要です。では、あなたは自分自身とハッピーでポジティブな関係を保つ方法を知っていますか？

　健康でいるためには自分自身のケアをしなければならないことは誰でも知っています。身体的にはさまざまな方法で自分をケアすることができますが、思考や感情についてはどのようにケアしていますか？　自分自身について考えるとき、あなたは自分にやさしいですか？　あなたは自分にやさしく思いやりのある考えを持っていますか？　あなたは自分のことが好きですか？　楽しめていますか？

　自分をケアするために何かをするのは良い習慣です。自分自身にやさしくすることは、自分との関係を大切にする良い方法です。やさしく親切にすることを生涯の習慣にするためには、練習が必要です。これは絶対に自分にしかできないことなのです。

99 *Speak Well To Yourself*

What you think about most of the time has great power in your life. You can change your thinking with how you talk to yourself in your mind; this is called self-talk. Self-talk is **the ongoing talk in your mind** you have with yourself. Self-talk runs from the first waking moment in the morning until you go to sleep at night.

Your thoughts and your self-talk are either positive or negative. You look at the world around you and what is going on and you either view it as positive or negative. Make sure your self-talk is mostly positive because your self-talk about what is going on will make you a positive or negative person.

'I have to be careful what I say to myself as my self-talk is the thing in my life that makes me happy or unhappy.'

Toni

---

the ongoing talk in your mind 心の中で行う自分との継続的な対話

99. 自分にやさしく語りかける

**自分自身に語りかける言葉、セルフトークは、
人生において大きな力を持ちます。そのため、
常にポジティブなセルフトークをすることが
大切なのです。**

【日本語訳】
　普段からどんなことを考えて過ごすかは、人生に大きな影響
力を持ちます。心の中でどんなふうに自分に話しかけるかで、
考え方を変えることができます。これをセルフトークといいま
す。セルフトークとはあなたの心の中で行う自分との継続的な
対話です。セルフトークは朝目覚めた瞬間から夜眠るまで続き
ます。

　あなたの考えやセルフトークはポジティブにもネガティブに
もなり得ます。周りの世界を見渡して世間で起こっている出来
事を見るとき、あなたはそれをポジティブまたはネガティブに
捉えます。普段からポジティブなセルフトークを心がけましょ
う。というのも、世間で起こっていることについてのセルフトー
クは、あなたをポジティブな人間にもネガティブな人間にも変
えるからです。

　「私は自分自身に語りかける言葉に気をつけるようにしていま
す。セルフトークは自分を幸せにも不幸にもするからです」

トニー

100 *Success Starts With You*

Success in a relationship depends on the way you think and care about yourself as well as how you think and care about the other person. A positive attitude about yourself is **one of the most important things** you can bring into your relationship. When you feel good about yourself you can then add something strong and **valuable** to a relationship.

Being happy and loving to yourself as well as the other person makes you a more balanced, happy person. When you like yourself and have a strong feeling of care and thought for yourself, you will have more care and thought for the other person **as well**.

---

one of the most important things 最も大切なことの1つ　　**valuable** 価値ある
as well 同様に

100. 成功はあなたから始まる

自分を大切にするのです。
そうすれば、
あなたは人にもやさしくすることができます。
自分に対してポジティブであることは、
人間関係においてとても大切なことなのです。

【日本語訳】
　人間関係がうまくいくかどうかは、相手のことをどう思い、どれぐらいやさしくするかにかかっていると同時に、自分自身のことをどう思い、どれぐらいやさしくするかにかかっています。自分自身に対するポジティブな姿勢は、人間関係にあなたがもたらすことのできる最も大切なことの1つです。あなたが自分に対して良い感情を持っていれば、人間関係に強さと価値を添えることができます。

　相手に対してだけでなく、自分自身に対してもハッピーで思いやりのある態度で接すれば、もっとバランスの取れた幸せな人になれます。自分を好きになり、自分自身へのいたわりと思いやりを強く持つことで、相手に対しても同様にいたわりと思いやりを持って接することができるのです。

English Conversational Ability Test
国際英語会話能力検定

● E-CATとは…
英語が話せるようになるための
テストです。インターネット
ベースで、30分であなたの発
話力をチェックします。

www.ecatexam.com

● iTEP®とは…
世界各国の企業、政府機関、アメリカの大学
300校以上が、英語能力判定テストとして採用。
オンラインによる90分のテストで文法、リー
ディング、リスニング、ライティング、スピー
キングの5技能をスコア化。iTEP®は、留学、就
職、海外赴任などに必要な、世界に通用する英
語力を総合的に評価する画期的なテストです。

www.itepexamjapan.com

日英対訳
恋と人生に前向きになる英語100

2021年12月4日　第1刷発行

著　者　ヴィッキー・ベネット

翻訳者　かとゆみ

発行者　浦　　晋亮

発行所　IBCパブリッシング株式会社
　　　　〒162-0804 東京都新宿区中里町29番3号 菱秀神楽坂ビル9F
　　　　Tel. 03-3513-4511　Fax. 03-3513-4512
　　　　www.ibcpub.co.jp

印刷所　株式会社シナノパブリッシングプレス

ISBN978-4-7946-0686-0